Don't Be Defined

By Tai Renee

To every black woman who feels like the weight of the world is on her shoulders.

To every black mother who knows what it means raising a black child in this world.

To every black professional who is trying to fit in and stand out at the same time.

To every black person who does not want to be defined by every choice they have ever made.

To all my friends, family and those who have spoken life into my ability to share; This is for you.

To the person who needs to be reassured that they are not alone; This is for you.

To the person who is seeking inspiration and motivation to keep going; Here's to you.

Introduction

The Blog, *Don't Be Defined,* was the prelude to this mini memoir. For many years, I had never really taken the time to consider who may be witnessing my life story as it unfolds. I failed to recognize that at times, I was being admired for my champion mentality.

I rarely stopped to contemplate who I might be inspiring. It did not dawn on me that I might be a role model to someone and that my willful determination may have had the ability to motivate those around me. I was engulfed in being a scholar, a strong woman, a mother, and a loyal and dependable friend. My body and my mind constantly remained occupied in my teenage and young adult years that I neglected to truly unpack my trauma.

Raised to be an independent woman, there was no time for self-pity or for pause. My goal-focused personality allowed for little downtime to dwell on any short comings I may have had. I continued to push through no matter the obstacle that was presented before me.

Over the years, I have received many messages, both written and in casual conversation from peers and strangers alike. Messages that detailed empathy, sympathy and genuine praise for how my life has turned out despite it all. Commendation came from acquaintances, close friends and sometimes people I had meet for the first time.

They spoke words of admiration, encouragement, and positive affirmations which initially, I struggled to embrace. Eventually, I began to become empowered by these comments. Compliments tend to make me feel uncomfortable. So, instead of immediately responding with a "thank you", I usually ramble to take the spotlight off me. I am learning to embrace these compliments and I am working on accepting the praise that I receive. Acknowledging that I have come a long way and that if someone else were to be faced with some of the same circumstances, their road may not have ended up where mine has taken me.

Another thing I did not considered, was how my story would have an impact on others. There were many times along the way as I shared some of my most impactful and hurtful moments with others, that they looked to me with tearful eyes. They appeared to be in complete awe of my life accounts as I testified my stories to them. They were viewing someone who had not been swallowed up by negative self-talk, depression or who had fallen deep into a trauma-infused hole.

For the outsiders looking in, as I picked myself up after each undesirable interaction, I could see how that could have an impact on those around me. I could only hope that they would use my strength as a catalyst for their own. I never sought out to be this person. But, as I have learned to live in my truth, I finally get it.

It took me a while to realize the magnitude of the obstacles I had overcome. For so long, I did not believe I was an inspiration to anyone. I did not think I was worthy of such powerful words. It had taken me a while to realize that the trials and tribulations I had triumphed over, could have drastically altered my life in so many ways. A downward spiral could have led me down a path of destruction. I am blessed that was not my fate.

One day, my mother and I were messaging each other. I do not recall what the initial conversation was regarding, but I was mentioning to her that I was considering relocating. My mother messaged me telling me that she admired me. My own mother. The woman who I looked up to. The woman who raised me and my sisters and who modeled for us what It truly meant to be a strong, black, independent woman.

I cried while reading the message repeatedly to myself. It was in that moment that I knew there was something amazing about my story; Something worth sharing. If my mother, who was my hero found it in her heart to admire my journey, there were bound to be others who would be as inspired.

For roughly a decade, I grappled with sharing my story. Sharing, entailed me being open and honest with others, but most importantly with myself. I would re-live some of my most traumatic experience and have them memorialized forever. People close to me encouraged me then to share and continue to encourage me now.

For the most part, I am a private person. Sharing my story would leave me open and vulnerable to the world. Then, I got to a point where I had to remember why I was sharing in the first place. Although my writings have been my own form of therapy, I was not only sharing for myself. I was writing for others who may have similar stories. My goal was always to empower women and to remind them that they are not alone. My goal through my writings was to motivate, to inspire, and to provide solace and support to those who need it so we can all heal together.

I finally settled on the notion that this is one story that people truly need to hear and *feel*. There are so many life secrets and unspoken taboo topics that have kept women in silence for centuries. Many painful topics addressed in this mini memoir should be spoken among all women.

Instead, they are pushed so far back into our memories they are often forgotten. They unfortunately are not shared with the young adults who need to hear them the most. These secrets, if spoken aloud, may shed some light for young woman and spare them having to learn some of life's lessons.

To be silent, is what many women know all too well. There is so much guilt and shame in many of our stories. There is so much pain in our stories and yet we sit in silence with our pain; acting as if all is well. We are raised to be strong, independent women, to never complain and to always find a way.

I share my story to remind the next woman that she is not alone no matter what she is facing. No matter the struggle, the barrier or the steep uphill battle, you are not alone. Hopefully, my story can be used as inspiration for the next woman to keep pushing forward, no matter how dark the road may look ahead. A story, presented to the world, to encourage the next woman that she should not, will not, and cannot be defined by her story.

Young Tai

The Persian Gulf war had begun. My mother, with my father by her side, welcomed me into this world. I was born in the middle of January. It was the middle of winter in Boston, Massachusetts, so I believe it is safe to say, it was a cold winter day.

My memory, mostly through pictures and shared stories, painted my early days with my parents, my older sister, and myself living on my grandparents second floor. My mother shares a story of me, as a very young child. My mother and my father were in a panic searching for me one morning. They could not tell my grandparents that they had lost one of their daughters overnight. Apparently, I had fallen off my bed with my pacifier in my mouth and my swishy jacket in hand and ended up underneath the bed. I believe it was confirmed then that my sleep mattered to me the most. Falling off a bed, being uncomfortable or cold, did not seem to interfere with my sleep.

There are pictures of what appear to be my older sister and I terrorizing our father while he slept. I am sure my mother got a kick out of snapping that photo. One of my favorite pictures is me and my mother at the beach. She is posing with me on her hip and with no caption to the picture, you can just tell I was a sassy and spoiled baby. Shades and all.

When I was three years old, my parents, my older sister and I moved to a small neighborhood of Boston. My mother was pregnant with my little sister at the time. When we first arrived on scene, I remember the street bustling with children. Particularly, there were children running in and out of the residence two houses down.

I have very fond childhood memories. My sisters and I did not want for much. There were some Christmas gifts that I put on my list, what seemed like annually, that I never received. I was fortunate to receive plenty of amazing and thoughtful toys and gifts; however, I am still sad I did never receive a power wheel. I ended up purchasing my son one for his first birthday and he could not care less about it. As a child, I would turn our living room into a town for my barbies. I used a block set we had, and I would interlock the blocks into squares to make houses, stores and structured streets.

As a young girl, I would watch WWE wrestling with my father until my eyelids became too heavy to keep open. He would tell me the sandman had come for me and he would carry me off to bed. Draped over his shoulder or nestled in his arms up against his chest I was the happiest girl. I would climb into bed with my mother and father early on a Saturday morning begging them to take my sisters and I to Chuck-e-cheese. I did get lucky every so often. My memories are mostly warm and happy.

There were times I remember my parents arguing, although I never knew what for. I tried to tune it out usually right before bed. I never felt like I had much to worry about, so dozing off did not feel like I was abandoning neither my mother nor my father. It was extremely rare that my mother raised her voice at us, and she never hit us. I remember my father being the disciplinary parent. A booming voice and a hard hand. But the way he spoke to me always felt loving and protective.

I was slightly afraid of my father. Around six feet tall, handsome, dark skinned, southern and loud, I only remember trying him once. I was packing my bag to go to my cousin's house. My father told me I could not take my barbies with me and that I would have to use my cousin's. I could not believe he would say such a thing. I needed to have my own barbies, dressed how I wanted them dressed, and you know, there is just something about playing with your own toys. I packed them anyway.

I am not sure if I was caught trying to also stuff my barbie car in my bag, or if he was doing a spot check, but I took a spanking for being disobedient. I can still feel my behind and legs on fire. Until this day, I am not sure if I ever received any other spankings from him, but that felt like my first and my last.

I am the middle child and I treasure it. Contrary to what people may assume about middle children, the syndrome they often allude to, I never experienced it. I liked to think of myself as kind of a loner. I enjoyed playing alone in the house. I do not recall seeking attention from my parents or my sisters. My father used to play basketball quite often and I vaguely remember being his nurse one day.

Hoisting his leg up on a basketball, tying it off, checking the pulse of his knee and then icing it. I remember singing in the car with my mother as we moseyed through the city or dancing to gospel music as we cleaned the house on Saturdays. Football was a staple in our house. After Sunday service, my parents would watch whatever games were on TV while I listened and played with my toys beneath their feet.

My best friend and her family lived two houses down. As I became older, I spent more and more time going back and forth between our houses. When the weather was nice, we spent as much time outside as possible. Riding our bikes, rollerblading, skating, racing, playing tag and manhunt, tossing around footballs and playing basketball at our neighbor's house. We stayed out until the streetlights came on. That was childhood law.

My mother was fortunate to place my sisters and I in the Metropolitan Council for Education Opportunity Program (METCO). METCO is a program that busses inner city grade-school-aged children to surrounding suburban schools to be provided a better education. This was an opportunity only select children were afforded.

There were many early mornings I remember showering with my eyes closed in preparation for school and napping on the school bus on the way outside of the inner city. The schools that I attended were predominantly white. In elementary school, I was unfazed race wise. I mixed and mingled with everyone. As I spent nights at friend's houses, I could see that their houses were bigger than my parent's house. Some houses had projectors and game rooms inside and others had play structures and swing sets outside. I never saw those in the inner city.

When middle school rolled around, I started to become aware of many differences between some of my previous friends and myself. I noticed that I had unintentionally began growing closer to other Black and Hispanic students from the inner city. We could relate to each other more and overall, we had more in common.

What I did not realize then, was that even though at the time I did not feel it, those of us who were selected to attend the schools through the METCO program were privileged. We were afforded any opportunity that other parents wished they could give their children. Attending a METCO school made some children feel as though those of us who attended were better than them, when that was not the case.

As a child, I felt burdened to have to get up so early and travel so far away for school. My grandfather stood at the bus stop waiting for us every day after school and brought us to his house for dinner. We did not get to our house until after five in the evening when my mother or father retrieved us after work. The days felt long. It did not at all seem worth it. There were days I longed to have gone to school closer. Attending a closer school meant being home sooner and meant spending more time with my local friends.

As middle school wrapped up, I remember not wanting to attend the town high school. I felt like I was missing out on what my own city had to offer. I knew very little people in the inner city, the way some of my other friends did, and I truly felt like I was missing out. I wanted to be able to build those connections locally as well. I did not know where young people really hung out and I felt like a visitor in my own city sometimes.

I was bussed to school during the academic year and off at overnight camp during the summer. I am still unsure if my mother did this to keep us busy while she worked, or if this was a tactic to ensure we would not spend too much time idling in the city streets. My parents had divorced right around the fifth grade. I am sure my mother would have had her hands full with three girls at home all summer long.

I know the divorce was hard on her and to this day, I have no idea how she managed it all. Working, keeping a home together, and being the primary provider for three children, I know could not have been easy. How my mother did it all without missing a beat and with no complaints still has me in awe.

I had taken an exam in the eighth grade with the hopes of scoring high enough to attend the top exam school in the inner city. Unfortunately, I did not score high enough for the top-ranking school so, my mother declared that I would continue traveling for my education. I initially was upset, frustrated and annoyed, but I was for the most part, obedient. I doubt I argued much about it though because at least there would be people at my designated school that I knew. The summer rolled around, and I was thankful to be free from schoolwork, free from commuting and free to work.

I Sent a Man to Prison

It was a warm day in June. It was also the summer before my freshman year of high school. I was fourteen years old. I did not begin my summer employment yet, so I was sleeping in. I had a bunk bed at the time and even though the bottom bunk was more convenient to sleep in, I always slept on the top bunk. The air conditioning was on blast and I was tucked under my thick comforter, yes even in the summer. I was asleep on my stomach with my arms above my head and tucked under my pillow. My head turned facing the window and away from the door.

My childhood home had two floors. On the first floor, upon walking through the front door, you entered the foyer. This area contained a coat closet and the stairs to the second floor. The basement door was situated in a small hallway leading to the rest of the house.

Immediately passed the foyer, was an open area with a desk, a computer and a bookshelf. To the left of this area, was the living room. To the right, was a dining room that we had converted into a bedroom. Towards the back of the house was another small hallway that led to the shared bathroom.

Directly across the hall from the bathroom, was my mother's and my bedrooms. They were side-by-side. To the back of the house, was the kitchen. The second floor had an open landing and one bedroom with a walk-in closet and a bathroom.

My sleep was abruptly interrupted when I felt some movement on my bed. Before I could fully wake up, the weight of someone else's body was on top of mine. Without hesitation, some sort of damp cloth was pressed against my face covering my nose and mouth. I could smell some unknown chemical as I began to struggle to breathe.

I attempted to scream, but my screams were muffled by the chemical cloth. I remembered that no one was home. Because if someone had been, this would not be happening to me. At first, I thought it was all a joke. I quickly realized that it was not, when the person on top of me did not release their grip. I instantly panicked as I was now fully awake, trying to gasp for air and without the ability to understand completely what was going on. I knew that I needed to fight for my life.

I shifted my body weight and placed my left leg on the outer side of the bunk bed to break the hold. We both fell from the top bunk directly on to the floor covered by rug. My view was obstructed by my comforter. I scrambled to gather myself and attempted to crawl to the door of my bedroom.

As I began to crawl, I soon realized that when I landed, I was not facing the door. In fact, after crawling a short distance, I had realized that I was facing the wall, which was on the opposite side of the room. I was far from the bedroom door. This became apparent to me when I reached out and felt my stereo system that was positioned up against the back wall. I sighed.

The comforter was now somehow wrapped around my upper body engulfing my head. The chemical cloth was back. It was in that moment that I figured that I was going to die right there, on my bedroom floor.

The weight of his body back on top of mine forced me to halt my fighting. I slowed and controlled my breathing. Something I had learned over the years being an asthmatic. I began to say the Lord's prayer like I was taught in church. I made it to the end of the prayer.

My head was pinned to the ground as I was balled up on top of my knees. A couple of seconds passed, and I was still breathing. I was still alive. That couple seconds of peace and that prayer gave me exactly what I needed. I began to make great efforts to break free.

He rotated me on my back, but at least this way I had a fighting chance with my limbs now available to me. Fear raged through my body as I knew what might be next. I began to kick and scream, and I tried to fight through the comforter. I felt a sharp pointy object in my side, and I stopped squirming. *A knife*, I thought.

He then pushed me underneath the bed. I began to squirm some more. I tried to free myself from the comforter to see my attacker, but he tightened the comforter more. The air conditioner breeze did not reach under the bed. It was getting hot quick and I began struggling to breathe again. *Air*, I thought, *I need air*. I stopped moving majority of my body so that when I slowly pulled the comforter from around my nose and mouth for air, it would not be noticed. I was able to breathe.

He began to rub his body, clothed with boxers, against mine. I was grossed out; however, I was now thinking about survival. I started to reach out to feel my attacker. I grabbed his head trying to figure out who it might be. My mind was racing trying to find any leverage on my attacker.

No hair. Bald head, I thought. At this point I knew it was not my older sister's boyfriend who often came by in the mornings while he was waiting for her to get out of class or finish at work. My sister's boyfriend had a head full of thick, long hair. *Could it be my neighbor?* I then thought. Since I recalled him constantly pacing the street. I did not remember hearing anyone break into the house. I then recalled that the air conditioner was loud so I probably would not have heard anyone break in anyway.

Next thing I knew, fingers were being forced inside of me. I cringed. I was hot, I was tired and if I wanted to stay alive, I knew I needed to be smart. After a few minutes, I was pulled up off the floor with the comforter still wrapped around my upper body.

At this point I was thankful he did not penetrate me with his phallus. My mind began to race as to what might be next. I began to give a little push back.

In a struggle, I was physically escorted out of my bedroom. I could hear the water running in the bathroom that was only paces away from my bedroom. The panic and anxiety were back. My mind immediately went to *he is going to drown me.*

I began to fight again. The stupid comforter was always in the way. He pushed me into the bathroom while I was screaming. The comforter became trapped in the door. Half of his right hand was inside the door, gripping the doorframe. I recognized the nails.

It was confirmed that I knew this person. I tugged on the door to get out of the bathroom, but I was not stronger than him. I wanted to see him now more than ever. I began to tell him that my mother was on her way. That she would be here soon and that he should leave now.

He let go of the door and I stumbled back into the bathroom. I pulled the comforter out of my way and I leaped out of the bathroom. My eyes darted through the dimly light hallway until I could make out who he was.

When I saw the man in front of me, I hysterically began to cry. I was in complete shock. Tears filled my eyes, and I was struggling to breathe again. I had no idea how I was still standing and had not collapsed onto the floor.

A man who had access to our home and someone my family trusted. My heart sank. He rambled on and on about how he and my mother had found my diary and they had read about boys that I liked, teenage girl thoughts. He mumbled something about how he was "showing me something" and how he and my mother had agreed to teach me a lesson.

What he was trying to show me, I would never know or ever understand. He was seated on the chair at the computer desk, in the open area beside the living room, dressing himself while he spoke to me. He seemed to be trying to explain his behavior. I remember being almost speechless. I was trying to process all that had just taken place. He was my mother's fiancé.

He left. My heart sank and my tears were back. I climbed into the shower, trying to wash him off me. I remember watching television shows where they would always tell the victim of sexual assault not to shower for fear of washing away any DNA. I always wondered why they would want to potentially wash away the evidence that would help put their attacker in prison.

In this moment, when I was now the victim, I got it. No one is thinking about the conviction and preserving evidence after you have been assaulted. You are thinking about trying to cleanse yourself of the dirtiness that you feel from having been sexual assaulted by someone you gave no permission to ever touch you.

Not long after my shower, my mother texted me asking me to move his clothes from the washer to the dryer. She was unaware that he had even been by the house. I texted her back and told her she needed to come home. She came home immediately. I explained to her everything that happened, and she took me to the hospital. I subjected myself to a rape kit and subsequently charges were filed. I provided my statement to two female detectives the day of. Feeling so strange in that cold hospital room. I went home that night. Feeling unsafe to sleep in my own bed, I slept in my mother's bed.

That night, after all the adrenaline had left my body, my entire body ached. I was loaded up with ibuprofen because truly every part of my body hurt. The next morning, I remember looking in the mirror. My face was blotchy from the chemical cloth and was raw to touch.

I was laid up in my mother's bed, full of pain medication, when my father called. He was in such a great mood. He asked me how I was doing. I lied and I told him I was doing well. Tears slowly streamed down my face while he told me about his day. I kept the conversation short so he would not be able to pick up that I was crying. I chose to not disclose to him the incident that was still so fresh on my body. I knew that if I told him what had just happened to me, my father very well might have ended up in prison and I am sure, would have never forgiven my mother.

My first- and only-time riding in the back of a police cruiser was to travel to the courthouse to give my statement to the Assistant District Attorney. There was no trial, but I would have testified if I had to. He was sentenced to seven years and one day. Mentally, I moved on from this trauma, like nothing ever happened.

I began my freshman year of high school and never looked back. I am not sure I ever really dealt with this trauma. In the beginning, any chemical smell was a trigger for me and caused panic to resurface. One day, I was removing nail polish from my nails and that is when it hit me. That was what was placed on the chemical cloth to try to sedate me. This trigger slowly subsided when I realized that I could begin to re-associate that smell with nail polish remover and not that traumatic encounter.

It would not be until years later that I would realize that I was far from alone with this experience. During the time of the incident, the lead up to his sentencing, and even him going to prison, I felt somewhat alone. I had family and friends around me that loved and supported me, but at the time I did not know anyone personally who had gone through what I had. It could be fair to suggest that I might have known someone, but since very few people talk about these types of incidents, I felt alienated. I pushed the assault to the back on my mind.

At some point, my mother put me in counseling. I hated attending. I would go afterschool, so I had to leave my friends in order to attend. My therapist was nice, but quite frankly I just did not want to talk about it. I do remember one session, which may have been my "breakthrough" session. I finally broke down and cried. I have no clue what specifically made me cry, but I had realized that since the assault first happened, I had barely cried or even sat with my feelings. Being candid, I did not want anything to do with it.

There were some people who did not believe me when I explained to them what had happened to me. I had a hard time trying to fathom why someone would think I would make up such a traumatic event. I tried to understand what I would gain from running with a story so heavy. It felt so strange to not be believed.

Unfortunately, a lot of people who have been sexually assaulted never come forward for this reason. For not being believed. Going through something so traumatizing and then being re-traumatized when your story is not believed, is heart wrenching. Thankfully for me, there was DNA that the hospital was able to collect, and the court was able to prosecute my attacker. The conviction, I believe, was the reassurance for the naysayers. Regrettably, not everyone has a favorable outcome.

At my young age, I did not really understand how this one incident could have drastically changed the trajectory of my life for years to come. I was strong, and I was not going to let someone else's actions control me. Trying to forget about the incident completely allowed me to continue with life, like nothing ever happened.

Also, having my attacker convicted and in prison gave me some solace. While he was in prison, I wonder if he would ever send someone to harm me. I wondered for a while, when he was released, if he would ever come to look for me. I wondered if he was sorry and if he regretted his actions. I will never know. All these years later, I have accepted that I will never know the answers. As more years passed, I realized that the answers to these questions no longer mattered to me. He did not matter to me.

Miscarriage Woes

At sixteen, I attended a scheduled doctor's appointment with my mother and younger sister. We were receiving our last dose of our recommended Human Papilloma Virus (HPV) vaccine. By far, the most painful shot I have ever received. The doctor told me, due to age, that she needed me to provide a urine sample for a pregnancy test. I provided it as requested. Shortly after, she walked back into the room and told my mother, my younger sister and I, that I was pregnant. I almost fell out on the floor. I was in complete shock.

I am sure you can only imagine the look on my face and my mother's alike. I had been sexually active, but I had been sure to use protection. I could not believe this was happening. Pregnant, and this is how I had to tell my mother. Us finding out at the same time was not ideal.

After my appointment, I shared the news with a few of my closest friends and my boyfriend. I did not know what to feel. My boyfriend did not know how to feel.

After a few days to process everything, I came to terms that I was going to be having a child. I was still early on in my pregnancy so there were no major plans that needed to be made just yet. I still needed to process everything. I began imagining life with a baby and how that would look while being in high school. I knew immediately that I was not going to be a high school dropout and that I would do everything to ensure that I continued to receive good grades. I considered how having a baby might change some of my friendships and hoped that it did not. Excitement began to set in.

It was only maybe a month later and I had gone to use the bathroom. Shortly after sitting down, I felt a decent size mass being expelled from my body. Unsure of what it was, I checked the toilet. All I could see was a large bloody mass. I panicked and called my mother upstairs. She quickly jumped on the phone with the doctor's office and we were on our way to the clinic.

I lost the baby. I had a miscarriage. The doctor was explaining to me what had taken place. She was educating me on hCG levels, the hormone related to pregnancy, and how mine had dropped. She noted that my levels would continue to drop as my body terminated the pregnancy. I remember tuning her out. In just one short month, I was imagining my life with a child and now I was imagining my life without a child. Can you picture the emotional rollercoaster I was on? An unknown pregnancy at sixteen and then a miscarriage. I was not prepared for any of this.

When I found out, I called my close friends over and cried about it for hours. The next few days were tough. I was trying to come to terms with the rejection of the baby. After those rough few days, I quickly moved on. I was young. There was not a community of people I could converse with to comprehend or talk through what I was feeling. To be honest, all of it was a lot to handle emotionally. My feelings were all over the place. If I am being candid, I am not sure that I did ever truly deal with the loss of my baby.

It was within months that I learned that I was pregnant, again. I think subconsciously, part of me wanted a do-over at motherhood. My boyfriend and I were still using protection, but it went from all the time to most of the time. The same way I had then went from not even considering a child, to not caring if I were to become pregnant. Silly teenager thoughts. Mentally I was trying to wrap my head around losing a child. I was trying to comprehend why I would lose a child, since I was so healthy and young. I knew in my heart, that I could be a great mother. So, when I became pregnant again, I was excited and prayed that I did not lose this child. I had liked to think at the time that there was no way I could lose two children. Pregnancies all tend to be on a case-by-case basis. The first pregnancy was terminated.

In hindsight, I would like to think that it was what was best for the child. With my second pregnancy, I was able to conceive and bring to full term my son. Maybe the pregnancy that terminated itself, would have not provided me with a healthy child.

The miscarriage was something that came to mind from time to time. Although, no matter how many times the thoughts and emotions resurfaced, I never spoke about it. There is a certain level of shame that comes with a miscarriage. I no longer blame myself, because I knew that I had done nothing wrong; however, there is a part of me, as the carrying mother, that tried my hardest to understand why my body would reject a pregnancy.

I am noticing a theme arising. Another trauma that I never appropriately dealt with. Because I was able to conceive quickly after the miscarriage, I pushed the miscarriage as far back into my memory as I could. It was simply, a thing of the past.

Growing up I wanted to have two children back-to-back. A boy and a girl and then I vowed I would be done. When I became a teenage mother, I knew that it would not be ideal to have my children so close in age. So, I gave that thought up.

Over the years, I subconsciously believe that I may have been scared that I may not be able to carry another child. The thought of losing another baby would have been too detrimental to my mental health. As I reached my mid-twenties and my son had become more independent, I knew that giving birth to more children was not in my future and I truly became just fine with only giving birth to my son.

Fertility issues are such a taboo topic. Unfortunately, it is rarely talked about but experienced by so many women all over the world. There are so many women who suffer from multiple miscarriages and some who have the inability to conceive at all. It truly is a traumatizing experience. No matter the length of the term of pregnancy, the trauma is naturally still the same. To know that your body rejected a child, is an extremely tough burden to bear.

A lot of us were made aware of abortions in our teenage years. I am sure we all knew someone who had one. Others know some women who had multiple. But when I was a teenage, a miscarriage was foreign to me.

My doctor did advise me, at my follow up visit after losing the baby, that miscarriages were common. She also suggested and that there was nothing, especially that early on, that I could have done differently. Can one truly find comfort in that statement?

The older I get, the more women I know that are struggling with or have struggled with infertility. It is more common than we all know. I have a strong suspicious, that women are not openly speaking about infertility due to feeling ashamed. There is also this fear of judgement.

Women are raised to complete this fairytale of being married and bearing children. For those women who struggle to have children, they tend to go through waves of emotions which can include sadness, anger, devastation, hopelessness, loneliness, feeling ashamed, and being embarrassed; just to name a few. They are ashamed that they cannot conceive and carry a child like many women have been programmed to want to do.

Sometimes women consider decisions they made in their past, whether it be abortions or years of birth control, that they rationalize to have caused their infertility issues. Some women regret not having children younger, as their body is now going through hurdles trying to conceive.

Sadly, the overwhelming list of thoughts women have trying to comprehend their infertility is lengthy. Couple these thoughts and feelings with the parents and friends, alike, who are plotting on every women's womb. Consider waiting until you finally meet the right person you feel comfortable with to bring a child into the world, only to find out that children may not be in your future. Think of the homes that become broken when the union cannot conceive.

Another stressful conversation leads us to women who use abortions as a means of birth control and women who are blessed with children but are incapable of raising them. Imagine being the women who struggles to conceive a child and witnesses a mother unfit or unwilling to take care of her child continue to be blessed with children.

I support a woman's choice; I want to make that clear. The ongoing debate is almost always around the women who abuse their right to abortions because they refuse to take other measures to protect themselves. For all the women who struggle to get pregnant and have children, I am sure we all can imagine what that could feel like and how unfair it must feel. To have a body capable of bearing children, complication free, and for someone to abuse the right repeatedly.

My miscarriage woes resulted in a healthy pregnancy followed by a healthy child. For others, it never will. Every so often, my mind drifts back to the child I lost. Did I lose a girl, a little mini me? Would my life be any different than it is now if my first pregnancy went full term? I sometimes think that maybe the miscarriage was a second chance to not be a teenage mother. But being a stubborn Capricorn I wanted my chance at being a great mother and I did not care if I was jeopardizing my future to do so. No matter the price, no matter the struggle.

I also think that if I did not have the scheduled appointment and had passed a bloody mass one day, if I would have even known that I had lost a baby. More than likely not. It also leads me to wonder, all the women who have had miscarriages who never even knew they were pregnant.

We all have our secrets. This was one of mine for a very long time; However, I hope that things change and that women talk about these situations more often. Miscarriages and infertility are not things to be ashamed of.

Unfortunately, they are not uncommon. When people constantly harass women about having children, suggesting that because they are married or because they are older or whatever reason people think that they should have given birth by now, remember that many women walk with internal trauma related to conceiving. From having trouble conceiving completely, to miscarriages, to stillbirths, to disabled children, etcetera.

Even for the mothers who carry children full term and then experience post-partum depression. Bringing life into the world is one of the most selfless things a person can ever do. That great gift also can come with considerable weights.

Women, we need to discuss these things more often. Conceiving, miscarriages, abortions and parenting. This might be my miscarriage woe, but this is another woman's desperate cry. Let people live on their own terms, for you know not what they go through. The women that I personally know battling with infertility issues are some of the strongest women I know. To want nothing more than to bless the world with a child and to have a chance at being an amazing parent. To have done everything right and to have the burden of possibly not being able to bear a child. Please be respectful, be kind, and be considerate.

I was Seventeen

If I remember correctly, it was around two thirty in the morning. The pain was unbearable. So unbearable that I woke up ready to scream. I laid in bed for a few more moments before I texted my mother, from my second-floor bedroom that I had move to when my older sister left for college.

When I could get myself together enough, I crept down the stairs and into my mother's bedroom. I crawled into her bed, rolling from side to side in agony. I remember telling God, aloud, to "just take me". I was seventeen and my son was ready to enter the world.

When I could, I walked the short distance from my mother's bedroom to the bathroom and sat on the toilet bracing myself for the contractions that were coming five minutes apart. I showered in record time. Four-minute shower to be back seated on the toilet to brace myself through my next contraction.

My mother drove the speed limit, stopping at every red light to the hospital. My mother had called my boyfriend before we left the house, so I called all my friends from the car. I left voice messages that I was on my way to the hospital and that we would have a baby soon enough.

My mother parked the car and wheeled me inside in a wheelchair. When we made it to the labor and delivery floor I stood up at the large doors and walked the rest of the way into the room. Nurses and doctors came in to check on me and prep me for delivery.

I knew from watching birth shows throughout my pregnancy that I would not be giving birth without an epidural. I was then escorted into my private room where I would remain until I gave birth. The on-call anesthesiologist came in to administer my epidural. I was given instructions to remain still. That if I moved during the administration of the epidural, and the needle hit a nerve, I could become paralyzed. Very scary information to hear for a teenage who was also in grave pain during contractions. I made sure to take a deep breath and then somehow managed to hold it in as to not move while the needle was inserted.

With my epidural in place, morphine became my best friend. I lounged in the bed, morphine pumping, while I made additional phone calls to friends. I remember watching snapped on TV while I was in and out of sleep.

At some point, my son's fathered appeared at the hospital. I remember waking up to greet him. There were a lot of nurses and doctors rotating in and out of the room checking me and the machines.

At one point, a doctor came in to break my water by puncturing the amniotic sac. My contractions began to really jump off the chart and sleeping became more frequent for me. There became increasing pressure on my lower body and soon the pushing began. I gave birth to a healthy baby boy after eleven hours of full labor and only eleven minutes of active pushing. coincidently, my son was also eleven days late.

About a month prior to giving birth, I left school to do independent work from home. I utilized tutors for the reminder of my junior year and went into school for test taking purposes only. For me, it was not ideal for learning, but it was necessary to maintain my grades and to be able to complete the school year.

It was difficult sometimes, to understand the material I was expected to learn on my own and to be motivated to complete work and not just play with my son all day. But there was never a time that I considered dropping out. I knew that my future was too bright to leave school and that I could never be trapped in a position, having limited ability for professional growth. I knew that the best way to ensure security and stability for me and my son was to complete high school and attend college.

My dream of working in the criminal justice field had not dissipated, it had only intensified. Since a teenager, I knew that I wanted to work in the criminal justice field, particularly as a probation officer. I was unsure the path I needed to take to make it to this destination, but I knew that I needed a solid education to make it there.

I also knew, that furthering my education would open many doors for me and that it would not solely limit me to probation. I fully recognized now that I needed to make my dream my reality to ensure that I could take care of my son.

I remember feedings at three in the morning. They oddly were my favorite. I would snuggle my son and peek at social media. I would spend my last monies on diapers and gas constantly budgeting and re-budgeting to make sure my son had all that he needed. Sometime after my son turned five months old, me and his father had broken up. I was focused and driven, and my son's father was not. Unfortunately, my son's father was unable to provide much for him financially. He gave money when he could, and both of our mothers bought necessities here and there. But the bulk of the financial burden fell on me.

I maintained my employment at a supermarket, after my son was born, and it gave me great flexibility with my school schedule. There were times where I occasionally appeared in school during my senior year, extremely tired and smelling like baby spit up. I was encouraged to join a newly formed mother's group while I was pregnant in my junior year.

Our guidance counselor felt it would be nice for the three of us to meet. The group consisted of a mother of a one-year-old, another pregnant student and me. Personally, I did not see much value in the group. I see what the thought process was, around support in numbers, but to me it felt forced. I had support in family members and friends already, so the group meetings felt more beneficial for the other two mothers than it did for me.

When I came back in-person for my senior year, I was asked to re-join the group. One of the girls was pregnant again. She advised that her birth control had failed her. The other girl reported that she wanted to get pregnant again in order to have her children close in age. This honestly did not feel like an appropriate space for me. My focus was on raising my child, of course, but it also was on ensure the best future for both of us and that did not include having additional children as a teenager. I could sense that the minds were not the same in this group. I had so many plans for my life and always vowed to let nothing and no one get in the way. So, I left the group.

Some would suggest that I made being a teenage mother look easy; maybe even fun. I barely slept many nights in the beginning, but I made it to school and work every single day. At this time in my life, I could not stand the taste of coffee, so how I was able to function those days were purely just relying on my youth.

I also was sure to toss in a few nightly activities with friends on the weekends just for kicks. At seventeen, it felt easy. Being so young and so full of life. I had the responsibility of being a mother but love and assistance from my family and my son's father's family that I will appreciate forever. I had to grow up faster, to take care of another human being, but I was still fortunate to be able to enjoy my teenage years.

There was never a doubt in my mind during these years that things would change at some point. Recognizing that there were many teenage mothers that were not fortunate to have the support that I had. I did not take that for granted. I knew that I was blessed, and I appreciated the love and the support that my son and I both received.

I knew how it looked to the world, being a black teenage mother. The comments, the looks, and the hardcore statistics. I did not let those things interfere with what I knew would be my future. Having a child at seventeen for me, meant I just had to work twice as hard as the next person. I had to fight through lack of sleep, work more hours than I wanted and constantly shift my schedule, but never my focus. If I was going to be a statistic, I was going to be one that would blow everyone's mind, even my own.

"The Privilege Walk"

It was my senior year of high school. I was back in-person in school full time. It was springtime and my English teacher was extremely excited to play a game for one of our classes. She grabbed her pieces of paper, which included the instructions and questions I presume, and she relocated class to an open hallway space within the high school.

Our teacher had all of us stand side by side in a horizontal line. I still recall the excitement on her face. She began with giving us the instructions. We were to listen to the following statements that were read by her and to follow the instructions that were given. We were also advised that this activity was to be done in silence. It seemed easy enough.

Our teacher read off statements such as: if you grew up in a two-parent household, take one step forward, if you have a learning disability, take one step back, and so on. The silence made the questions feel like daggers. Watching classmates move forward and backwards around me was reassuring, eye-opening and anxiety ridden. Requesting us to step forward and backward, with having the option to not move at all if we did not feel comfortable.

It was very intimidating. There were some students who never had to take a step back. They ended up at the finish line. At the conclusion of the exercise, she asked that we look around and see where everyone had ended up on this journey. There were only three black students in my class, including myself. None of us made it to the finish line during this exercise.

It was a very quiet walk through the hallways back to class. I deduce many of us were trying to comprehend how we were feeling after the exercise. When we returned to the classroom, we all sat quietly in our seats.

My recollection is of me looking around the room and gauging others facial expressions and any outward emotions while sitting with my own feelings. I felt very uneasy. I noticed that there were white students who were ahead of me but also white students who were behind me. I could not help but notice that the three black students were nowhere close to the finish line.

It was a weird concept to me. Putting everyone's business out there like that and without our permission. We were judged, emotionally naked and I did not like it.

Our teacher broke the silence. She stood at the front of the classroom and asked for our thoughts, prompting us with questions that she must have had on her papers she had with her. There were some students, who ended up close to the top, who felt good about where they landed on the privilege walk. There were some students who realized their limited privilege.

I heard some students who strongly felt that if people simply took control over their lives they could be just as privileged. It was a suggestion that everyone could be successful and a statement that emphasized that the people who were not successful, or further along on the privilege walk, were just lazy.

I could see the other black students in the class shaking their heads and disagreeing with the remarks of the white students who were too privileged to understand how their words were degrading and affecting those sitting in the classroom with them. I remained silent. I had a lot to say, but unsure of whether it was worth it to say anything. By many of the comments that were made, I was not sure that majority of my classmates would even understand my point of view. They had seemed to already have made up their minds, that obstacles were self-made.

It was when a classmate said that people who get pregnant make a choice to do so. This was after he had alluded that people who did not do well in their classes were lazy and did not put in the effort to receive good grades. I had reached my limit and I finally broke my silence; I snapped.

I was screaming with tears in my eyes as I began to refute all the insults. I explained to my classmates that I was in an AP statistic class and that I was currently receiving a D. That I was staying after school a couple times a week for extra help and I still was not getting the material.

Unfortunately, it was too late in the semester for me to transfer out of the class, so I was forced to basically figure out a way to not receive an F. I then refuted that females do not always "choose" to get pregnant. I expressed to the entire class that I had used protection when I had gotten pregnant with my son and for people in the classroom to pretend like they were not sexually active was beyond me. I also pointed out to the white classmate who made the statement that he, as a male, would never have to physically deal with that burden of becoming pregnant. And, if he did accidentally get a female pregnant, the heaviest of the burden would be on her to continue with, or make the decision terminate the pregnancy.

It was the arrogance for me. He truly believed that none of these things could happen to him. That he was invincible when it came to life obstacles. By the looks of many of my classmates faces, I had realized that many of them did not expect any of what I had to say, but they also had never been forced to take their white privilege lens off. It was the unintentional disrespect from classmates that I had enough of. Their privileged lives, their easy upbringing and lack of obstacles that did it for me. It was the judgmental eye. He appeared to be looking at some of us through his microscope from the highest realm of privilege.

He did not acknowledge the classmates who had learning disabilities and the idea that this might be something out of their control. Or the households that had separated at no fault of the children. The list felt inevitable of situations and circumstances some of my classmates appeared to know nothing about. A world outside of their small town seemed to not exist.

At some point in my rant, the teacher from the classroom next door had run down the hallway to get the principal involved. Our teacher stopped them at the door, signaling to them that she had things under control. It was not long after my rant was over that class had ended. I grabbed my things and left. I do not recall if my teacher had made attempts to assuage the situation any further; however, if she did, it had no bearing on me. I just know that in the moment, I wanted out of the classroom.

My memory of this day was very vivid for a while after. I devoted a lot of mental space to thinking about this whole incident. I still remember this scenario in my head, a decade later. In a sense, I felt like I had opened the eyes of some of my classmate who clearly were wearing blindfolds. Some of these classmates I had gone to school with since the first grade. They were so privileged that they never noticed the struggles of the inner-city students. Shoot, it appeared they did not notice the struggles of even some of the classmates who resided in the same town.

For me, it was waking up around five o'clock in the morning and getting my son and myself ready for the day. Doing a daycare drop off before driving approximately forty-five to an hour to get to school. Other students who lived in the inner city, were taking multiple buses and multiple trains to get to school all to obtain what was said to be a better education.

I do not believe it was the experience of the exercise that was the most eye-opening part for some of my classmates. I truly believe it was not until those of us who chose to share our own stories, putting names and faces to struggles, obstacles and barriers, that made some classmates hear us.

That had been one of the many battles that I fought in high school. I remember being the only black student in some classes and being asked to address the class on slavery, a topic that I was learning right along with everyone else. I remember being too tired some days to even engage in conversation.

In hindsight, I wonder if I was too tired or if I just did not care to enough to entertain the questions and the comments regarding black culture. Exhausted of constantly having to teach people who did not look like me, what it meant to look like me. High school was when the differences of ethnic and white classmates truly began to become prominent. Knowing that I was receiving a good education was reassuring but now it seemed like at the cost of not only having to be the student, but also having to be the teacher.

I was constantly having to explain the differences in my life to my classmate counterparts. For example, explaining to them why I discontinued running track so that I could work more hours during the school year, while other students were able to engage in sports during every season since having a job was not a necessity for them. Or how I had to study overtime to ensure that I made good grades to even be considered for a top college.

I am not sure what my teacher took from the class that day. In some ways, I think it was an eye-opener her for as well. I do not think she expected the class to go that way, but that was also her own privilege. I was not upset with her honestly but, years later, I can recognize that she was not equipped to host that class. She did not anticipate or seemingly have the knowledge of the potential hurt and trauma that could and would be caused doing an exercise such as this one. I know that she had positive expectations of the exercise, because of the person that she is.

Unfortunately, she neglected the fact that she would now have to close the wounds that she opened for some of us. I do not resent her or blame her for this encounter. I do recognize that she was trying to address race, inequality and privilege in what probably seemed like a fun and creative break from our high school essay writing and college preparation. Her own privilege got in her way. I truly hope she received a lot from that experience and if she used that exercise again, I pray that she conducted some research on the closing segment.

People will judge you, period. But more so, they will judge you for what they know nothing about. They will use their privileged lens to try to understand someone and neglect, that for some people and some situations, you must remove the lens and look with fresh eyes. The goal should include having a willingness to learn others. It should not be waiting until someone has reached their breaking point that you are willing to hear them out.

This also taught me to always speak up. As frustrating as it might be to explain my life choices and my struggles, it is just as infuriating to know that there are still people who are unable to see the differences in others and are unwilling to recognize why these differences are important.

It also must be understood that some people are simply unintentionally ignorant to what they have never known or may have never been exposed to. I like to think it is not my purposes to explain everything to everyone but, there are some instances where we all should consider that the only way some people will learn, is if we create the inception of the education.

It is not fair to judge someone for not getting to the finish line as fast as you got there. It is commendable that they make efforts every single day to get there. Even when they may fall short, acknowledge that everyone's walk is not the same.

I appreciate the efforts of my teacher. Her attempt at trying to include important topics in class does deserve some kudos; however, I encourage people to be cautious of opening people up to be vulnerable in these types of situations.

When you do this, you must then be able to assist people in processing their trauma, providing them some comfort and then pacifying their pain. There is training that goes into these types of exercises. For some people, they do not realize that they are doing more harm than good. Because this was a classroom experience, with little insight on the student's part prior to engaging in the exercise, we had no idea what we were setting ourselves up for. We had no say in our willingness to participate.

For me, this had me hurt, angry, frustrated, but also seemingly added more fuel to my fire that I would have to be successful. Not just for me, not just for my son, but to prove that I was not just a statistic and that I had a lot to offer the world. That I was not just some black girl who would work a minimum wage job and end up on government assistance. That I was not lazy and that I would work hard for everything I deserved. I could not believe how ignorant some of my classmates were, but they did not know me, and it truly showed.

I was empowered and wanted nothing more than for people to see me and truly see me. Not to see me as a black girl from the inner-city, not to see me as a teenage mother, not to see me as someone having a "story to tell" but to see me for who I was outside of the trauma and stereotypes. Seeing me, Tai, a young woman with a vision and the determination of many men. This same year, I was accepted into a prestigious university. I could not wait to show out in the fall.

I Cannot Help You

Freshman year of undergraduate school, I was nervous, anxious, and excited all at the same time. So many thoughts raced through my mind. *What if the material was hard for me to comprehend? What if it was difficult for me to make friends or fit in because I was not staying on campus? Would I still be able to work and attend school?* I was excited to begin the next chapter in my life, but I also was worried about the unknown.

I was honored and felt privileged to be attending such a prestigious university in Boston, MA. My son and I continued to live at my mother's residence. The university was located a short distance way in downtown Boston. Living at home was comfortable, convenient, it allowed me to save money and it afforded me the support of my family that I would need through my college journey.

I attended the orientation, prior to the first day of school, and I felt comfortable and confident locating my classes when the semester began. It was suggested, to all students, that we should keep an open mind early on in our education when it came to identify a career path. I took heed to this advice as I did not want to pigeonhole myself in a specific career track. The thought was that if I initially began with an opened mind, I would be able to accurately identify my true interest. I knew that my curiosity was in the criminal justice field. I selected sociology as my major with a crime and justice concentration. This way, I would be able to receive a broader understanding of human social behavior, including relationships and social interactions, as well as social constructs, order and change.

One of my first classes in undergraduate school, I recall a white student complaining about the five-page paper we had been assigned. She was expressing that five pages seemed excessive and that she did not feel prepared to produce the paper. I looked at her with a confused face and thought to myself, *five pages? What essays had she written in high school?* I was unsure if she truly felt unprepared, or if this was a tactic to use her privilege to get out of doing work. I learned quickly that it would be a little of both.

I encountered a few other students who had similar thoughts and concerns as this classmate. They appeared to have been accustomed to having done less work in high school and seemed to have been able to talk themselves out of assignments in the past. It was noted that they were strongly uninterested in doing much work for their education and that was a shame.

In the first semester alone, many students had expressed feelings of stress and anxiety regarding college expectations and stated that the pressure of the assignments had begun to build up. Some students seemed to truly have difficulty with nailing down a major, attending classes, and completing assignments. They were struggling with the seemingly unlimited freedom college brought.

Over the following semesters, several students shared that their parents were paying, out of pocket, for their education. The way some of my classmates were switching their majors every semester, or not selecting a major was baffling to me. Some classmates were not doing well in their classes. Not because the assignments were tough, but because they refused to attend class. Some of my classmates discontinued attending a few of their classes and just sent in assignments during the semester; many of them being late.

I was attending college on student loans. There was no option for me to not identify a major, to miss classes or to not complete assignments. I recognized that there was no one to save me if I did not receive good grades in order to maintain my financial aid and additional scholarships. There was no one who was going to assist me with the burden of paying off my student loan debt if I did not graduate in four years.

The students, who were attending on their parent's dime, did not seem too concerned if they failed a class or ended up needing to complete additional semesters. There was no need for them to work while they were in school; they were provided an allowance. There was no rush for them to complete their degree in order to solidify a good paying job. A job that would allow them to take care of their growing child, pay their bills, and receive relevant work experience all while paying back their student loans.

I did understand the demand on students, as there was a demand on me as well. For those who previously lived at home with very structured environments, I could see why they were struggling to assimilate into the abyss of college life. But the privilege some classmates had, did not provide them with the same urgency in being successful in college.

Whether they wrote the five-page paper or not, or whether they extended their college experience beyond the four years did not matter to some students one way or another. They would be provided a way to be successful, no matter what their work ethic or abilities resembled. The more I wanted to do well in school, the more I realized the importance of taking on the right responsibilities and only the ones that felt right.

My statistics professor and academic advisor indicated that she was doing a research project during one of our meetings and asked if I wanted to participate. She assured me that it would be a group project and that I did not have to join the group if I did not want to. She did note that it would be a good experience and a resume booster for me if I did choose to participate. I accepted her invitation and I put in a request to join the research group.

Over the upcoming summer we were to watch crime TV shows of our choice and to identify themes throughout the shows. We would then showcase and present our research and findings in Washington D.C. I learned all of this at the first meeting. Initially, it sounded reasonable.

But, as the summer progressed and I worked more, I was not pulling my weight with getting my research sent to the group. I was working as many hours as I could, and I was taking care of my son. I tried to make time to spend with friends and I realized that I was neglecting my responsibility in the research group. As I thought more about the intricate details of the trip, I recognized that I would be responsible for my flight, lodging, food and getting around the city.

After careful consideration, I sent my professor an email and indicated that I could no longer take part in the research group. I could tell she was upset by my revelation through her email response. I was slightly confused since there were at least four other students in the group. It also was not last minute that I was withdrawing. There was time to ensure that the project was well put together even with me leaving the group.

Personally, I did not think it was appropriate for me to request money from my mother for this trip *and* ask her to watch my son all while she was a single mother of three daughters and had two grandchildren living in her house. My professor allowed me to separate from the group. Being freed from the project gave me much needed relief. I enjoyed the summer until it was time to get prepared for the fall semester.

The following semester I enrolled in an internship and job readiness course. The professor of this course indicated that she would assist us in obtaining internships and prepare us for the workforce. She provided all students a list of places that she and the university had connections with for internship opportunities. She also told us to provide her with first, second, and third choice options.

My professor asked that I speak with her after class. She informed me that she would not be assisting me in getting an internship. She stated that she had heard how I did not follow through with the research project over the summer and indicated that she did not want to damage one of her connections if I did not follow through with the internship. I explained to her that the project was an extracurricular activity and that this was a graded course. I also explained to her my financial barrier with the trip. She did not see the difference and stated that she could not jeopardize the connections that she, and the university, had worked tirelessly to build.

Hurt and frustrated I left her class. I initially wanted to drop the course. The negative energy had rubbed me the wrong way, and I was unsure whether I would be able to be successful in her class if she already had a certain perception of me. I had to remind myself that this course was pertinent to my future.

This course would assist me in building early connections for potential job opportunities, support me in narrowing down my employment focus and it would allow me to receive experience in my field before graduation. Another booster to my resume, it would aid in my ability to secure employment, which I needed, right out of college.

I tried to convince myself that I would not have time for an internship anyway since I was enrolled in school full time and employed for at least 20 hours a week. But I refuted this false narrative assuring myself that I always accomplish what I put my mind to. This course would assist me in determining which career route I would pursue when I graduated. My last thought was, *I will do it myself and I will do a dang good job.*

I spoke with my mother, whose employment was affiliated with the Department of Youth Services. After taking a course on Child and Adolescent Development, I quickly realized that the juvenile population was my new focus and who I instantly became passionate about. My mother was able to connect me with a site director who accepted me as an intern. I could not wait to attend class to tell my professor that, without her help, I was able to secure my own internship.

I was not going to allow her, or anyone else, to force me to withdraw from this course. I took my future success seriously; I would do whatever necessary to put me in the best position to be successful. This felt like a life win for me.

It was at this moment, that I recognized that I was never going to take *no* for an answer when it came to my success and that I would always work hard for what I truly wanted. When I advised her that I had secured an internship, she appeared to be happy for me. I am not sure if initially it was genuine or not, but nonetheless, she did not have to have her name attached to my failure or success. That was fine by me.

This was my reminder to not get discouraged. People and objects are put in place to distract you, to throw you off, and to see how bad you really want something. I think I wanted to show my professor that I was capable more than I even wanted to take her class! Telling me to secure my own internship was simply a test at how bad I wanted this.

There are different versions of the middle finger. Her having to give me an A, was mine. During the early days of attending the course I was upset with her and unsure how our relationship would be throughout the remainder of the semester. I realized that at the end of the day, I did what I needed to do to stay in the class. She turned out to be a very good professor and I truly enjoyed taking her class. Ultimately, we both got what we wanted.

Do not give people the power to determine your success. Most importantly, do not allow them to block your education, your growth or your blessings. I made my internship work for me by rearranging my schedule. I ended up truly enjoying my internship and my professor had many valuable nuggets to offer us. To me, this experience was not just about the class. This was my introduction to my field and my future. I almost gave up, and I am grateful that I did not. It was then that I realized that I would always have to work hard for what I want in life. This was just the beginning.

Toxic

I was single and the feelings of loneliness were beginning to creep in. Of course, my friends were a staple in my life, but I was missing having a significant other to go on dates and spend nights talking on the phone with. I was in my junior year of undergraduate school. I was working as many hours as my school schedule and home life responsibilities would allow, but I was still feeling this emptiness of being single.

I had gone on dates here and there and had some casual conversation with some young men over the phone; however, nothing had panned out. One day my male best friend at the time, had called me and asked me to give him a ride. When I arrived to pick him up, he had been walking with a male friend of his. His friend took an interest in me, and after a few messages back and forth I had agreed to take him up on his offer of a date.

When I brought this information to my male best friend, he had become upset and annoyed that I would even entertain his friend. He warned me that it was not a good idea. I took this warning with a grain of salt and told him that I appreciated his concern and him looking out for me. I advised him that I was still going to pursue things and see where they went.

I was unsure whether my friend was giving me advice with my best interest at heart, or if he was jealous that I was not interested in him. I do not make it a habit of considering that any of my male friends have any interest in me. In this case, it was how upset he had become over the mere mention of the potential relationship. He seemed more bothered than concerned.

I wanted to take heed to the information that he had shared with me; however, in my loneliness and singleness, I also wanted to give the young man an opportunity. I was twenty years old and unfortunately still had the naïve mentality that if I was the perfect girlfriend, I would be able to win them over.

The relationship had already begun with red flags. Many of them I tried to ignore. It turned out that he was a reckless individual. He had a loving and caring way about himself, but he also had a devious and manipulative side to him as well. He lied about almost everything, and he lied often.

I continued to be drawn in more and more by my own need and desire to be a great and supportive girlfriend and became fixated on being able to change him. The more I attempted to assist him in wanting to live life the right way and on positive terms, the more emotionally attached and involved I became. At times when I should have been creating space, I was over analyzing how I could make things better between us. I was, often, neglecting what I needed while also sacrificing my desires and values to make my relationship work.

Before I knew it, I had begun to rapidly lose sight of who I was. I was now in an extremely toxic relationship and I allowed it to turn me into someone, over time, I did not recognize. Everyone else could see it, but I tried everything in my power to act as if things were fine. To seem like I was in complete control, even though I was gradually falling apart.

I did everything I could to be what I thought was an amazing girlfriend; like women are constantly told to do. I even altered some of my values, my standards and myself in order to make things work. I had not realized that I was losing pieces of myself. I was drowning and trying to climb out was getting harder and harder.

I made numerous excuses for him. Telling myself that he just needed time to turn himself around, reminding myself that he loved me and making attempts to justify his actions and refute the naysayers. I truly wanted my relationship to work. I was not ready for another failed relationship. I did not want to be single again and start all over with someone else.

We had been living together and, for a while, sharing my vehicle. He assisted with babysitting my son and to disconnect from him just felt so hard. I somehow began to sink into a depressive state. My relationship was extremely exhausting and draining. I was finishing up school and working two jobs, with one sometimes being overnight. I needed a break, and I did not feel like I could get one. I knew that I had to keep pushing through, for just a little while longer, so that I could move on to the next chapter of my life.

After almost two years of being in the relationship, I woke up one day and realized that when I was a little girl, dreaming of my future, I had not envisioned my life this stressful, overwhelming, and unhappy. I began to realize that I needed to discontinue the relationship. The amount of stress and financial strain the relationship was causing me finally had brought me to my limit.

I knew that for me to transition to the next chapter in my life, I needed to be mentally, emotionally and physically free of the disaster I was calling a relationship. For almost two years things had not changed for the better. I would wake up in the mornings wondering if we were going to have a good day or a bad day.

Every time he called me, I wondered what situation I was going to have to assist him with getting out of. I was done and I needed to part ways. Living together, I knew that this would be harder than if we had not been. Nonetheless, I was ready to have full control of my life back.

One night, we had gotten into an argument about yet another lie. I had basically had it. I was cold, distant, direct, and knew the end was near. He was officially on borrowed time. I was over the argument as it was going nowhere, per usual. I began getting ready for bed. I was tired after working a double shift. I knew that he was going to continue to lie and at this point, it did not matter what story he was attempting to sell me, I just wanted to get some sleep.

He was playing a video game on his gaming system and had refused to turn the volume down. For a short time, we went back and forth about the volume. He had blatant disregard for my need of sleep and used the volume as a childish and petty antic to punish me for not believing his tale. My recollection fails me with what exactly I said that pushed the button, but when I get to my boiling point there is no stopping the hurtful things I may say. There is never an excuse for what transpired, but I do know how my mouth can get.

He was seated on the opposite side of the queen bed from me, close to the TV, while the conversation regarding the volume was taking place. I had been at the other end of the bed in a seated position. In the blink of an eye, he lunged across the bed. He grabbed me by the face and mushed my head backwards pushing the back of my head into the wall. With his force and the weight of his body, we both fell to the floor.

He then, picked me up by my clothing and placed me on the bed on my back. He quickly climbed on top of me pinning my arms by my side with his knees. The weight of his body was on my legs. I tried to break free with no luck.

While the tears welled up in my eyes the rage and anger appeared in his. I took a deep breath to calm myself and to take a second to think. This situation brought me back to previously being assaulted in my own home and not having the ability to free myself from someone else's hold. I then remembered that we were not alone in the house. I screamed at the top of my lungs.

His face changed to panic as we could hear footsteps below us running towards my second-floor bedroom. He climbed off me. Seconds later my mother and younger sister burst into the room. That was the last straw for me. It had to be over.

As crazy as it might sound, this ended up being one of the best lessons of my life. I was at one of the lowest and most vulnerable places in my life, and arguably one of the worst places to be. I was lonely before I entered this relationship and because of this, I had given someone else power over my happiness. I allowed a relationship to dictate my happiness and I thought if I just worked so hard to be great and keep my relationship together, I could in fact be happy.

I began losing friends and I came up with excuses for why they did not want to be around me. I wanted so much to not be lonely, but coincidentally I felt more alone than ever. No one ever wholly knew what was going on in my relationship. I barely wanted to share. Some weeks and months the bad outweighed the good and this was how I justified why I stayed. I felt like I had nowhere to turn.

I truly thought one day the man I loved so much, would wake up and realize how amazing of a person and girlfriend I was. But I had to realize that it was not me, it was him. No matter what I did, or how great I was, he was not ready and ultimately, he was not for me. I was already this amazing person and it was not my job to continue to remind him of that. It was his job to see it.

It took me unfortunately, almost two years to realize this. In any relationship there will be obstacles to overcome; however, the strength of the relationship should not be dependent upon someone's blatant disrespect for the relationship and the other persons willingness to sacrifice themselves to stay. A relationship is as strong as the people in it make it and staying with someone by manipulation or through multiple levels of toxicity does not add value or strength to the relationship. Someone who loves you as much as they claim, would care so much about you that they would never subject you to certain things.

I was able to experience one of the worst examples of a relationship. There was a lot of giving on my part, and a lot of taking on his part. Do not get me wrong, there were sweet date night moments, and valentine's day gifts, but nothing, that overtime, could combat the lows of the relationship.

Experiencing this type of toxic relationship allowed me to build a better foundation for my relationships that would follow. It allowed me to adjust my standards. It allowed me to be demanding and vocal about things I would not and will not put up with. I became strong enough to end the relationship and strong enough to figure out what I truly want out of any relationship. Being at an all-time low like I was, reminded of a place that I would never allow myself to get to again.

I remembered that I had full control over my life and my happiness. I refused to give anyone that much power over me or my happiness ever again. I vowed to never be that weak again. This was twenty-two months of my life. There were times I felt completely alone. I felt as though I could not really share what was going on within my relationship as I knew I would have been judged. I prayed that he would get it together but ended up having to remind myself that this was not unconditional, healthy love. This was damaging to me and my mental health.

I also had my son to think about. This was not the role model I wanted for my son. This was not the mother I wanted him to see and thankfully his exposure to a lot of the drama was very limited. My son needed to see me as someone who was strong and would always having his best interest at heart. I needed to rally around my own self and remember that despite all, my future was still too bright. I was refusing to let anyone dim my light. The biggest void during this time was the absence of my best friend.

My First Soulmate

Some people have multiple best friends while some people do not have any at all. Some people change them every few years and some people have a bond so strong, that they almost become the same person. My best friend and I finish each other's sentences and have, in the past and even now, been confused for sisters. Sometimes actually, we have been mistaken for each other.

Several years ago, I put my best friend in an extremely tough situation. There were things going on in my life that she did not agree with and I allowed our disagreement to interfere with our then, twenty-year friendship. I was too consumed with what I had going on that I just tabled our issues and made do.

The initial disagreement had stemmed from my toxic relationship. She wanted me out of the relationship that I was not ready to give up on. In other words, I had not seen the light yet. Time went by and it continued to eat at me; us not being as close as we once were. My other close friends were great; however, things were just not the same. I missed my best friend.

The issue that was keeping us apart, for the most part, was the fact that I was continuing to be in a toxic relationship and continuing to ignore the red flags that were presented repeatedly. As an outsider, and as someone who knew me extremely well, she could not understand why I would give someone the power and ability to change the trajectory of my life. Why I would give someone so many chances that always resulted in me being disrespected and disappointed. Why I was not being the strong woman she had known me to be all these years.

I did not have any answers for her, since I was dealing with many of these questions on my own. Trying to comprehend why and how I had gotten here. There were other friends in my corner who were supportive; they just wanted me to be happy. Realistically, genuine happiness was not possible in this relationship. In the back of my mind, I believe I knew this myself.

I invited my best friend out to one of her newly favorite breakfast restaurants one Saturday morning. I honestly was surprised she had taken me up on the offer. I was nervous and anxious about how the conversation was going to go. We are so much alike that I already knew how painful this conversation was going to be.

We started with just casual conversation, lightly catching up. I knew at some point I would have to cut to the chase. I began by illuminating my faults and apologizing for my wrongdoing in how I handled things when it came to her and myself. I never discontinued speaking with her, I just made sure that when we did speak, I never spoke of my boyfriend or my relationship. I figured it was easier that way. Over time, she grew more and more distant and there was an unspoken understanding of where we both stood.

I alluded to how long we had been friends. Her response and tone, implied that the length of our friendship was not going to dictate our friendship moving forward. I quickly processed this reaction and realized that our friendship was hanging on by a thread.

I do not know who started crying first. I then began to plead for my friend to reconsider our friendship. There was just no way she could not be in my life. She had been in my life since I was three years old. She was not just my best friend; she was my family. I explained that I am no role model, that I understood where I went wrong, and that I was still working on myself. She stopped me to say, "You never know who looks up to you".

It hit me then. That people were watching me, including my friends, and that they had nothing but love in their hearts for me. They could see the things I blindly could not see. How could I have been so senseless?

How could I not realize that my life choices had a direct effect on other people's lives around me. It was this situation which led me to realize my importance to the people around me. The people who knew me inside and out and the people who knew how hard I had worked to be a great friend and mother alike.

I had almost lost someone who is extremely important to me and destroyed a friendship that has been an everlasting staple in my life. That pain of separation from her was one of the worst pains I have ever felt. It was worse than any romantic break up I had ever had in my life. She truly is my soulmate.

There were other friends in my ear constantly asking the status of our friendship and I honestly think they were hoping that if she and I were no longer friends, they would be filling her shoes. This was a friendship that I needed in my life. This was a long-standing relationship that I needed to continue to withstand the test of time. I needed to remind myself that she always has and will always have my best interest at heart.

Through my darkest moments, my toughest decisions, and my greatest achievements, I have always been able to call on her. As someone who cherishes family, friendships and loyalty; Our friendship means the world to me. She really is my family. She has always been a sounding board, a listening ear and someone who I know I can sit on the couch with and talk for hours, or travel to the most beautiful land and bask in the sun.

Almost losing my best friend was extremely tough for me. It would have been much harder if I were not mature enough to realize that I was wrong and that it was on me to start the dialogue for us to heal and to amend our friendship. I hear people often say that they do not need a certain friend or that they will just find another friend. People seem to think that authentic friendships are seemingly replaceable like everything else. People are so quick to end a friendship instead of working differences out.

A true friend is extremely hard to come by. This was a huge personal growth moment for me. It was genuine and it was hard work. I appreciate that she knew what our friendship meant to her as well. She knows my heart. She knows me. That was one of the toughest years of my life I would say, but a necessary year, nonetheless. Our separation made me much stronger and gave me a new appreciation for everyone in my life.

Friendships are some of the strongest bonds that we have. Friends are who we share our deepest secrets with, they are who we call in time of need, who we cry and who we vent to. They are the gatekeeper of our most embarrassing moments, and they are who truly know and understand us. Friendships are necessary and vital for happy, healthy, and successful lives.

Karma's Hold

Have you ever woken up one morning to realize that you did not love someone anymore? This was me and it was cold. I woke up one morning and realized that I was no longer in love with my son's father. It felt like all the love that I had for my son's father dissipated or at least was somehow transferred to my son.

When I thought about it, it appeared to be a slow and steady tapper of my love through the pregnancy and after I had my son. My son's father did not have the same drive that I did. Even that young. This seemingly forced a wedge between us, unbeknownst to me at the time.

Fast forward several years, I felt the love fade from my, then, relationship. My boyfriend at the time had woken up one morning and had a similar wakening I had. It was cold.

They often talk about this notion called karma. If you have not met her yet, you most definitely will. She does not play around, and she comes when you least expect it. She does not always come in the same form that she was dealt in, but she has a way of humbling you quickly and not always quietly.

She appeared and I was beyond confused. I do the breaking up, it is rarely the other way around. Initially we were in love. Him, I felt, more than I. He began showing me a life through a relationship that I had not experienced before. He constantly wanted me around his family members and friends, and we felt very good together.

For the first time I had moved out of my mother's house and we leased an apartment together. It was not long after the moved, I had begun to think about marriage and our continued future together. The relationship started to decline on our one-year anniversary.

We got dressed up and went to a nice dinner a few towns over. We sat at dinner, talking about our future. The conversation regarding purchasing property came up and we began talking about finances. He questioned mine. He noted my student loan and credit card debt and referenced how much money I spent on my son regularly. I will state, some of the credit card debt he referenced was from the furniture that we purchased together for our apartment.

By the way the conversation was going I could read that he was beginning to consider me a liability in his future. He never came right out to say it; however, his line of questioning and his snide comments told his true thoughts. I was hurt and perplexed. I had always pulled my weight in the relationship. I had always made sure the bills were paid and that there was food in the house. I had even bailed him out financially from time to time. It appeared that now, with his finances more in order, he was considering mine to be a problem.

So, to be questioned about my abilities felt demeaning. I also became frustrated because I always made things work, no matter what. I took those feelings, sat with them, and moved on as we continued with our night.

This appeared to be the turning point in our relationship. When people made comments to us about marriage, he made it known that he was not married. He questioned whether marriage was in his future. One night in bed, I told him if he did not see marriage in his future, then I could not be in his future. I always knew that I wanted to be married and if someone was unsure of that, and what also felt like unsure of me, there was no need for us to continue to waste each other's time any longer. Shortly after that, God severed our tie.

I quickly learned though, that this break up was more about him than it was about me. He was not ready for what I was ready for and his words, not mine, "we are not on the same page". He was right about that.

When we talked about property, he was talking about income property. He was not talking about a single-family residence for our family. He was not even talking about purchasing the residence together. When we talked about future children, he was unsure if he wanted any or when. None of our plans had lined up anymore and it was apparent that we were not on the same page. We had slowly become distant over the next year and it began to feel like we were just going through the motions out of convenience.

I went through many different levels and waves of emotion after the breakup. I was losing a friend who I was planning on spending the rest of my life with. I was losing a part of my support system. I was also losing someone who was paying half of the bills with me in our apartment. The apartment and bills that I knew I was not going to be able to pay alone for long.

I began to panic wondering how I was going to be able to do everything on my own. I began applying vigorously to new job opportunities. The following month, I was blessed and fortunate to accept a new position and agreed to a fifteen-thousand-dollar salary increase. I knew that I had to choose me, and then prayed that everything else would work itself out.

When my mind finally cleared from being clouded by overwhelming thoughts and my emotions settled, I woke up one morning realizing that this outcome was one that was going to work in my favor. Not only was cold hearted Tai back, but the Tai that works extremely hard under pressure and is determined to always make it work was also back.

I reminded myself that things only fall apart for other things to fall into place. My stress began to fall off me and I knew that my path would realign. I had faith and drive and that combination in the past always led me to my rightful destination.

I began my new position and was able to take care of all the bills, solo. More blessings began to pour into my life. It was not that this person was holding me back in any shape or form, but something was holding me back. It was not time for me to get comfortable, which I had been. I had envisioned this life with this man, and I was not looking far enough out. I was not thinking big enough.

I had just finished graduate school and now it was time for me to get back to be a force to be reckoned with, and I did just that. I was a black woman with two college degrees from a prestigious university. I was still so young and needed to use that to my advantage. I was never going to settle for where I was. That drive and fire in me never turned off or died down. But I was too young to be comfortable. Being forced to be uncomfortable ignited a huge flame inside of me and I was not going to give up. Moving back to my mother's house was not an option and the brat in me was going to get my way.

After seven months in this position, crying on the phone with my mother feeling alone and stressed out with the job, I was able to plaster my master's degree on my office wall at my dream job. My cousin sent me a posting for a probation officer position and I almost did not apply. One night, after a long day, I knew I needed to toss my hat in the ring; so, I did. That flame inside of me was going to burn for a while, and I was going to keep fanning it to do so.

You may think that you have everything planned out. Things may seem great and so close to perfect. But realize what is not for you. Do not beat yourself up over it either. You get one chance at life and if something is not suiting you, you can and should walk away.

It felt cold of me to walk away from my son's father all those years ago, but I was not happy in that situation. If felt cold for my ex-boyfriend to walk away from our future together, but it was not for him anymore. I respect it. I must respect it. I respect people who can be strong enough to not waste anyone's time.

He knew when the relationship was not suiting him anymore and I was knowledgeable enough to give him the out. And he took it. He was strong enough to say, this is not for me. I later was able to see it as two people who had served their purposes in each other's lives. Our time together and relationship had an expiration date, like many things to. God needed things in my life to change for me to be where I am today. For that, I am thankful.

Everything Falls on You

My son asked me one day "mommy, why do you always have to do everything?" I was frustrated and I responded back "I don't know, but I would like to know too!" I already knew the answer though, even though I was not going to have that conversation with him. As a mother, a good mother, many things fall on you. A father will assist, but for the most part, married, single, separated, co-parenting, whatever the situation is, majority of the burden falls on the mother.

We carry these little people in our bodies for around forty weeks. They are an extension of us. We will do any and everything in our power to make sure that they have everything they need, regardless of what we may need. Our sole purpose, after giving birth, is to love and protect our child. That includes providing the basics, such as: shelter, food, clothes, a loving environment, positive affirmations, and life lessons, while also recognizing that the list is infinite.

So, when my son asked me that question, he was alluding to the fact that his father does not do half as much I do and as he was getting older, he was beginning to realize that. I decided, a long time ago, to separate from my son's father. This brought me to my present situation, a single mother. When you are seventeen years old, you have no way of knowing where life will take you. My son loves his father, and they have a great relationship, but my son's day to day life, falls in my hands. Parenting is an around the clock job whether your child is in your presence or not. Even while your child is away you are constantly wondering about their well-being. A parent's duty never stops.

My son was observing, at that time, my frustration and could see that I was feeling overwhelmed. He was old enough to understand that the stress of making sure everything that needed to be done in his life, was all on me. That his father was there, and capable, but that I was expected to make sure everything always worked out.

Whether that meant finding money from nowhere, or over-extending myself, it all had to get done. Parenting is rewarding and demanding all at the same time. I do truly have a sweet child and he lets me know often that he appreciates me. It will not be until he is more than likely far into his twenties that he will truly realize and understand all the sacrifices I have made for him as a mother, but most importantly as a teenage mother. I am okay with that.

I begged him not to have any children until he is at least twenty-five years old and I made him shake on it. As life has settled and I have crawled out of the mess that I have made of my life in my early twenties, the stress and overwhelming burden of figuring it all out has finally subsided and the life that I have always dreamed about for my son and myself is finally coming to fruition.

It was not always easy; being a single teenage mother. There were plenty of nights that I cried myself to sleep trying to figure it all out for me and my little guy. Revisiting all my past decisions and reminding myself that I made the right ones. My decisions were always strategic, logical, rational and calculated so they had to be the right ones.

I watched as many of my friends traveled the world. They moved freely when they wanted, not having to worry about planning for a babysitter. There were days I was buying groceries on credit cards, not for the points, but because I did not have cash for the purchase.

I remember calling my mother crying and asking her how she did it. Divorced with three children, my mother always found a way to take care of the bills, put us in summer camps and take us on a family vacation every summer. She did this with three children and never once complained to us about it. How she did it is still beyond me.

Watching her strength and observing how she took care of us, and the house, always reassured me that I could always do what needed to be done because she had. This is truly when I begin to run up my credit cards. When it came to after school and trying to find two hundred dollars weekly for it, I had no savings to pool the money from so I charged my credit card for the remaining balance that I could not pay out of pocket. My son deserved to have a fun summer and he did not deserve to feel any stress of how it got done. I was frustrated with my situation, but I also knew that if I just kept working hard, soon and very soon, things would have to change.

The following year, I had been able to establish a savings account that ended up funding my son's summer clothes and camp. Again, I was frustrated, stressed and annoyed because I had worked too hard to build an emergency fund. After I vented to a friend about my situation, I had realized that although I depleted my savings account and felt like I was back at square one, I was not using my credit cards this time. That was already a win.

There were still so many plans for my future that needed to unfold. So many life goals that still needed to be accomplished. These things were not up for debate. I have never been that parent in which I suggested that I am who I am because of my child. Everything that I do, I do to better myself. My son is extremely fortunate to reap the benefits. He has never wanted for anything and has always felt loved and supported.

When you do things for yourself and for no one else, they feel so much better and well deserved when you accomplish them. You work your hardest because it means a lot to you. That is the greatest reward.

No matter what happens in life, what unexpected situation presents itself, use everything as motivation. Use your happiest moments, use your weakest moments. Was being a teenage mother always easy? No, it was not. Even being a mother in my early twenties had its stressful times. Nevertheless, no hurdle should be enough to deter you from being where you are destined to be. It might modify your route, or slow you down, but it should never be enough to cancel the trip completely.

A huge piece for me as well, was support. From family and from friends. If for some reason, you do not have a solid support system, seek one out. There are plenty of resources available. It truly does take a village to raise a child and I will wholeheartedly say that without my support system, this journey would have been harder, much harder. I had people to call and exchange scenarios with.

Occasionally I relied on my mother or sisters to pick my son up from school or camp if I was tied up with work. This also motivated me to continue to work hard and to pursue employment opportunities, that would allow me to have a life where I did not need to request assistance from others. I wanted to be in a place where I could comfortably do it all.

Some people become too comfortable with the level a support they receive without realizing, that as a parent your goal should always be to make the best life for your child and yourself in the same. Through your hard work, your life should be simplified so that your child and you can reap the benefits of your years of sacrifice.

My son has attended all three of my graduations. Only one of which I believe he remembers; however, he is aware of what hard work and determination look like. He knows what a dedicated parent looks like. He knows what expectations there are of him, and he has a slight idea of what it will take to get him to wherever his destination is.

Although, all my accomplishments selfishly were for me, he has been an eyewitness to my success and my journey. Being a teenage parent does not have to limit you from being a successful and positive role model in your child's life or being able to instill values within them. Having your child young and/or having your child outside of wedlock does not have a direct correlation of the type of parent you can or will be. Do not let anyone tell you any different. Do not let them put you in a box. It will always be the drive inside of you that will get you to your destination.

Having a child in both or either one of these situations will be harder, that is an honest admission. But the possibilities of your success can still be unlimited. My son is now a teenager. We have an amazing bond. We joke about things we see on social media; we discuss money management, and we vacation together. He truly has become one of my best friends.

The bond my son and I have is something so unique and special. I made sure that we would have a relationship where we both could be open and honest with each other. I always wanted him to feel comfortable to come to me for anything. My son knows how loved he is and how supported he is in everything that he wants to do, and I made sure to pour into him at a young age.

Despite all the uphill battles to get to where I am now, I never let my son suffer. I always made sure that he knew nothing of my struggles because that burden was never his to bear. My son seeing my success firsthand, has shown him a hustling side of me.

So now that I can spend so much time with him, he can look back and remember the days that I was not able to. Now, when my debit card chip is not read at Dunkin Donuts and I give them another card versus asking them to run it six more times hoping it will work, he knows that things financially are better (someone really needs to fix those card readers). He never has to worry about not getting the items that he needs or deserves. I can only pray that I can continue to make him proud to call me his mother. After, all these years, I do not mind having to do everything.

Know Your Worth

I once read in an article somewhere, that women apply to job opportunities only if they meet all the qualifications listed in the job description. Men, on the other hand, apply to job opportunities even if they only meet around half of the qualifications. Go figure. One job opportunity I had applied for, I met a little more than half of the qualifications. If the men were doing it and securing the positions, why couldn't I?

I had just received my master's degree and it was time to seek out new employment. I noticed a job posting for a management position in juvenile justice and I applied. After conducting some brief research, I had realized that this position had ties to where I had completed my undergraduate internship. With a direct contact in mind, I reached out to see if they could provide me with some insight on the position and if they could advise me on the best course of action in order to secure an interview. My contact was able to ensure that my resume made it into the hands of those who would be making the hiring decision. My opportunity to interview was secured.

I interviewed for the position and I was assured that I interviewed well; however, I was not awarded the position. They were looking for someone who possessed more experience in juvenile justice detention. This did not surprise me. I was not upset with their decision. I had the privilege of being able to sit down with decision makers, with hopes that I had left an impression on them. I was able to ask plenty of questions to figure out how the next time I saw them, I would be more than qualified.

Shortly after the initial interview, I was invited back to interview for another position in management; one I was qualified for. I did not get that job either. I was a little upset, because although I did not possess the specific experience they were seeking, I did have experience through undergraduate and graduate school, as well as multiple years of work experience with this population.

A few weeks later, I received a called from the man who was chosen for the initial position that I had interviewed for. This time, I was offered an entry-level position within the company. I was told I did not have enough experience for management. It was suggested that I could begin at an entry level position with the promise, with no concrete timeline, of being able to eventually move my way up to management. I respectfully declined this offer.

I knew my worth. I was not going to take any position below my desired salary. I also could not agree to a position that would not fit with my life as a single mother. I had not worked tirelessly through college to secure my degrees, only to start over at an entry level position. The two years that I had worked in nonprofit while I obtained my master's degree was already entry level enough for me.

About a month later, the day after my older sister's wedding, I received another call. The call was to request that I re-interview for another management position within the same company. I was offered the job.

The position was an adjustment for me and took me roughly six months to begin to master my role. One afternoon, I was in a meeting with my boss. Apparently, an extension of our company was not doing well, and upper management noted that there would be some changes that would affect us. I was informed, that the man who suggested that I did not have enough experience for a management position, was demoted. I was now tasked with showing him how to do my job! I was in complete shock. Inside I was squirming like a schoolgirl, on the outside I was as calm as a cucumber.

I had been in the process of accepting a new position elsewhere. For the next month or so, I trained my new counterpart. I accepted my new job offer and informed my boss, and my new counterpart, of my decision to leave the company and pursue another opportunity.

Days before I left, the man that had been shadowing me asked if we could speak briefly. We stepped outside. He gave me a huge hug and expressed how proud he was of me. He told me that I ended up being great for the job. He could not believe that, in such a short time, I had learned so much and was able to train so many others. He wished me the best of luck and told me I would do great.

Doors do not always open for a reason. I am grateful that I had been denied certain opportunities and that I did not settle. There was a reason I was not chosen for those previous positions. I was supposed to be exactly where I ended up. There are two lessons with this one:

First, always know your worth and make sure that others know it too. Knowing your worth means that you have the power to dictate and negotiate for what is best for you. Companies have positions to fill and their best interest is rarely about what you need, but about what they need. I could have given up when the first door closed. I could have settled for a position that was not in my personal interest. I had not worked diligently to receive two degrees to not be able to use them to my advantage.

Second, always remain humble. I was patient and I waited. And most importantly, I prayed. I prayed for what was for me and God delivered. I could have been pompous and righteous, having to train the man who told me I was not qualified for the position I had worked to be so good at. I had to remind myself, that I know what I am capable of; other people will not know it until they see it. I was new in the field and I had to prove myself. Point taken.

I learned that I always need to stay true to me. Sticking to my ultimate game plan will, more times than not, lead me to the winning corner. If I would have settled, it is unknown career wise where I would be now.

It is extremely important that you fight for what you know you deserve. Always know your worth, and ensure others know it too. This is not only limited to career success. This notion can be fashioned and tailored to every part of your life. You are the author of your story, drafting words on the page every day. It is up to you to dictate how your story will read.

Everyone has their own goals. Whether it be professional, personal, spiritual, or all the above they are your goals, and you are entitled to them. Other's goals may not align with yours and that is completely fine; however, do not shift any of your goals to meet someone else's and risk not meeting your own.

Daddy's Heart

It was my first day back in the office from attending a multi-day work training. It was a beautiful spring day, and I was ready to take on my Friday. It was around eleven in the morning when my personal cellphone began to ring. I looked at my phone, not recognizing the number, and contemplating whether I was going to answer the call. Strangely, something about the phone number felt familiar, so I answered, "Hello?"

"Hi. Is this Taia?"

"Yes."

"I'm calling regarding your father."

The conversation felt so airy. I was trying to sort things out. I immediately thought that my father had been arrested and that he was calling me to bail him out. In my mind, that was the only logical explanation that a random woman would be calling me about my father.

She proceeded to tell me that she needed me to come to the hospital immediately. She advised me that my father had suffered another heart attack and that things were not looking good. As she was speaking, I pushed myself back from my desk where I had been seated sifting through paperwork. I was listening to what she was saying, but my body was beginning to go into a panic. I was attempting to decipher the information she was providing me, but my mind was racing. I hung up the phone and bolted to a coworker's office to explain what was happening. In my aggressive jog across the office, I was attempting to get into contact with my older sister. She was not answering her phone.

I made it to my coworker's office where I then, burst into uncontrollable tears trying to explain to her through sobs, what was happening. She escorted me to one of the chairs in her office and I sank into the seat. I got out as much as I could in my attempts to explain to her what was going on. I called my brother-in-law and told him I needed him to get into contact with my sister. I then called my younger sister and explained to her what was happening and that I was on my way to the hospital.

A manager was thoughtful enough to call me an Uber assuring me that I was in no condition to drive. I ran back to my office and packed up my belongings. My mother, who was away on a trip at the time, could not be reached via phone call so I messaged her to call me immediately.

I was on the phone with her as I hailed down my Uber and climbed inside. I was a complete mess. I cried the entire way to the hospital. My driver gave me tissues as he frantically tried to get me to the hospital as fast as he could. I spent some of the ride sending out text messages to close friends and family members advising them of the situation.

When I arrived at the hospital, I sprinted to the emergency room. My father's girlfriend was standing at the nurse's station. She was waiting for me and looked distraught. They would not speak with her until a relative was present. She and my father had been in each other's lives for ten years. She was family.

We were escorted to a room that had a sign that read *family room* on the door. The surgeon, a nurse and another woman with a clipboard entered the room after us. The surgeon began to ask questions regarding my father's diet, exercise and overall health. He noted that he was the surgeon who operated on my father when he had his first heart attack, two years ago. This line of questioning I did not find relevant. I interjected to get us to the point of this interaction.

The surgeon then begun to explain that my father was at the gym when he suffered a massive heart attack. He was subsequently rushed to the hospital. When he reached the emergency room, he went into full cardiac arrest; his heart stopped completely. This type of heart attack is known as the widow-maker. The surgeon rambled on and all I could think was *if you are my father's surgeon, why are you wasting time talking to us?*

As he continued talking and asking my father's girlfriend questions, it dawned on me who the woman with the clipboard was. She was a social worker. My father was dead. She was there to support the grieving family.

The surgeon told us that he was heading upstairs to perform a procedure on my father to try and repair his heart. He kept saying that my father was "extremely sick". No, my father was not sick, he was dead. I had to get out of that room. I needed my sisters to get to the hospital expeditiously.

My best friend showed up first while my father's girlfriend and I waited on the cardiac floor. During our initial embrace, we both broke down. She lost her father ten years prior. Heart disease. My sisters showed up together. I explained that Daddy was in surgery and that the surgeon would provide us with an update once the surgery concluded.

Every time the door to the surgical side opened, my anxiety rose. After a couple of hours, the surgeon came out. He brought us to a separate room to explain the procedure he had performed on our father and to describe our father's condition. He proceeded to draw a picture of our father's heart, including all the prior blockages, the new blockages, the old stents, and the new stents that were placed in the arteries of the heart to improve blood flow.

I prefer that people get straight to the point with me. He wanted to tell a story; I did not have the energy for it. Another surgeon met us in the waiting room. He explained that they had placed our father on an ECMO machine. A machine built to circulate blood through an oxygenator, acting as an artificial heart and lung. We went in to see my father. His body was ice cold. He was laid out on a cold table in a dimly lit room. I hated every minute of it.

We left our father that night, after he was situated in his cardiac ICU room. I can attest that we were all feeling extremely drained and overwhelmed. The next day, which we deemed Day Two, we were very optimistic. My sisters and I had been taking turns sitting with our father in his hospital room from day until early evening waiting for him to wake up. Day three, we became hopeful. They lightened the sedation, and this gave us the illusion that he was responding to our voices. That trial was shut down within minutes and the sedation was increased. His body had not responded well to coming off the sedation. To be completely honest, that was the day I lost faith.

For the next seven days. I went through the motions every day: Getting up every morning, getting dressed and ready for the day, dropping my son off at school and making my way to the hospital to sit with my father and hope for good news.

For a while, there was news, just not necessarily good news. It was around day five or six that fluid began to fill my father's lungs. Around day seven, they began to question whether there was any brain activity. A neurological team came in to conduct some testing. They did not seem impressed. I would usually take the morning shift sitting with and talking to my father. His girlfriend typically arrived for the afternoon. After several days of only sitting in the hospital, I had started going into work in the afternoons for a few hours for a much-needed distraction. I was a complete zombie.

Sunday morning, as I was getting ready to head into the hospital, the lead nurse called and said that my father's kidneys were beginning to fail. I informed my sisters and my mother, and we all headed to the hospital. We called my father's girlfriend for a family meeting with his surgical team from a hospital conference room.

His heart was still leaking. The fluid in the lungs was blood. The neurological exam showed low brain activity. The kidneys were failing. My father would need a new heart. *Who was going to give him one when he would then need lung work and new kidneys*? I identified the answer to these questions at the door.

I knew that it was time to take my father of life support. My mother yelled at me saying that I needed to have faith. My older sister wanted more time, *maybe he's still in there, and he just needs more time* she pleaded with us. My younger sister left the room. We gave him more time. We agreed that if anything else changed for the worst, that we would remove him from the hospitals last ditch efforts to keep him alive.

Monday morning, the nurse called for the last time. She told me that the kidneys were completely going and that my father needed dialysis. I called my mother and sisters from the car. It was time.

The floor attending came over with a troop of people. She was talking, but she was doing the same thing everyone else was trying to do. Keep hope alive. She kept saying "there is a good chance". I stopped her in her tracks. "What are the chances?" I questioned her. They were 30-70. The odds were not in his favor.

He was skin and bones at this point. He was tired; I know he had to be. His regular nurse, who we built a bond with, ordered us a cart of sandwiches, desserts and water. We called everyone. We sat with my father until everyone who wanted to be there, had arrived.

They turned off his lung machine first. They clamped his blood supply. I walked over and gave him one last kiss. Before I ever left my father in person or before we ended a call, he always told me that he loved me. I whispered to him one last time *I love you* and sat down. 2:14pm, they called it.

These were the worst ten days of my entire life. Then came the funeral planning and that was a close second. I cannot tell you how I made it out of those three weeks without completely falling apart. My friends and family were crucial. My coworkers were amazing.

I replay in my mind often, the time I spent with my father after his first heart attack. The first time, he thought he was having severe heartburn from a burrito. I vividly remember laughing and joking with him just a couple of hours after he was out of surgery. I had to leave to tend to a few works matters and to grab my son from school, but I made it back to him around seven that evening.

I ate dinner while he chatted with me about any and everything. I soon realized that he was just trying to keep himself awake. I finally encouraged him to get some sleep. He needed the rest. He finally drifted off and shortly after, I left to head home.

Days later, my father told me that he appreciated me for staying with him that night. He admitted that he was afraid to fall asleep that first night. He told me that the first twenty-four to forty-eight hours after the initial heart attack were the most unstable and unpredictable. He told me that having me there eased his fear and gave him some solace.

That is what nearly broke me this second heart attack. My father died without family and love around him. Although he was not completely alone, as I suspect the EMT's and other medical professionals where with him, he did not take his last breath in the presence and comfort of his loved ones. Something that still is disheartening to this day.

After my father's funeral, I took the first flight out the next morning. I needed peace amongst all that I was feeling. I was in route to Grand Cayman Island. I was hurt, drained and was seeking something. What that something was, I was not completely sure?

After ordering a personal jerk chicken pizza and a rum punch, I realized that my stay was not all-inclusive. My bill was forty dollars. I called my older sister in tears. My emotions were all over the place. I was beyond stressed and overwhelmed. Everyone was telling me how crazy I was for traveling to another country alone. I did not care. The last thing I needed was to be around people. I just needed some space to clear my mind and to have a full reset. Having watched my father wither away, plan his funeral and be a sounding board for my family, I was exhausted and had nothing left to give. I was not there long, but I was there long enough.

For the first year or so after my father's death, I went to the gravesite regularly to be near to and to speak with my father. Sometimes, I would be extremely upset with my father for leaving us, sometimes I just needed to cry. Some days, I wanted to tell him about what was going on in my life. I would tell him that I hoped he was proud of me and that I loved him.

I felt cheated of my time with him. Who was going to walk me down the aisle at my wedding? I battle with my own regrets of not spending enough time with him. Not calling him enough. Some days, I still feel like I am sitting in the hospital room begging my father to wake up.

For our father's one-year anniversary my older sister and I got tattoos of the damaged heart my father's surgeon drew for us. The pain does not go away, it just gets different. The smallest things trigger memories, and the most random things make me want to call him. I never wanted to join this community, but here I am.

Spend time with the people you love. As much as you can. You have no idea how long you have with them. My father had his faults, but he was my father. I did not choose him like my mother did, he was chosen for me. My father loved me unconditionally and the love for him was always returned. I always saw the value of having my father. I truly believe that if he had a stronger presence in my teenage years, that I probably would not have gotten pregnant. There is something about a father's presence in a young girl's life.

The bond between my father and I had begun to grow stronger as I grew older. As an adult, I began to understand more of his ways, and I could give him grace for some of the choices that he made in the past. It seemed like just when I was ready to truly work on our relationship, he was taken from me.

I do not believe my father died happy. I do not believe that his purpose was truly fulfilled. My father had his three daughters who he cherished, his grandsons who he adored and his mother who meant everything to him. However, he did not have much more than that when he passed. This realization truly hurt my heart, but I know he had so much more living to do. He had so much more to share with us and so much more to give to us and that was stripped away. Having him, taught me many life lessons and losing him taught me almost the same.

The Other Side of Friendship

There is another side to friendship. As we make friends during different stages of our lives, whether be it school, at work, in church, at the gym, through mutual friends, or wherever, friendships can be giving but they also can be strenuous and sometimes draining.

In the past few years or so, I had been regularly evaluating my friendships. This was prompted by an increase in disagreements, misunderstandings and miscommunication that I was having with friends. It led me to make efforts to try to better understand what the root cause of these negative experiences was. It even led me to evaluate myself.

I believe it to be important for me to give myself space regularly to recharge. This typically allows me to pour back into myself for me to be able to be available for others. During one of my re-evaluation periods, I had focused on some of the previous disagreements I had with friends. I had realized more about myself than anything.

I had learned that I was growing, and it was not always at the rate of others. That in the past, certain things may not have bothered me, but years later, they were now driving me crazy. I spent more time with myself and less time with others. So, when I was around friends, I noticed things much quicker.

As time had passed, some friends had unintentionally locked themselves into certain boxes and as my priorities, vision and routines changed, it was evident that not everyone could fit anymore. My life focus was shifting and unfortunately, that was not happening for all of those around me. I began to feel as though I was being pulled into this box with them, when where I was heading had no walls or ceilings.

I had also realized that sometimes, I spoke too much. I would interrupt people with feedback without fully letting them get their point across. Other times, I would share too much of certain habits the person exhibited or emphasized issues that probably should have been mental notes and not shared intel. Sometimes, I noticed that I was not listening enough. I was hearing what my friends were saying, but I was not always listening to understand what it was that they were expressing to me. I was giving them the free airtime, but I was deficient in assisting them in identifying a solution to their problem.

I realized all the times that I had failed to communicate effectively how I was feeling in certain moments. Always trying to avoid confrontation or awkward conversations that I was not ready to have. I would not be upfront regarding my feelings and I did not always ensure that deliberate conversations were happening.

When I feel overwhelmed or frustrated, I tend to shut down and ignore people. Evading and avoiding certain conversations and conflicts until I truly feel like I can completely process everything that has taken place. I like to give myself time to be able to identify what I think is an appropriate plan to move forward. I can see how my approach to dealing with conflict could allow some people to believe that I do not care about how a situation is affecting them.

As I have grown as a person, I have realized that it is truly beneficial for me to distance myself from certain relationships and to evaluate the ones I feel are most important to me. Some of my friends I know that I can call in the middle of a crisis for immediate assistance, some of them I can only grab drinks with. Although we may play catch up every couple of months, the friendship itself may already be in a box.

Some of my friends, I can party with and some of them I can sit with and talk until the sun comes up. I have some friends that I can travel with, and some who will cook for me just because I asked. But the friends that I can do all the above with, are the friendships that I hold the dearest to my heart and the people I have noticed that I have grown the closest to.

Over the years, I have learned that each of my friends adds a different value to my life. The more I learn about myself, the more I learn how to best interact with each one of my friends in order to preserve our friendship or how best to limit the friendship or disconnect completely. I thank God for my friends every single day.

I thank my friends, as often as I can remember, for putting up with me. I know that friendships go both ways, and I can truly be a lot to deal with. I can be moody and hard to deal with at times but, I also give good advice and will drop anything at any given time to be there for every one of my friends. There is always give and take.

Nourish your lasting friendships. It is important that you have supportive and emotionally healthy people surrounding you in life; However, be open to the fact that some friendships and certain relationships cannot coincide with who you are becoming. The other side of friendship is also knowing when the friendships has run its course.

We sometimes must accept that some friendships are for simply a season of your life. What I have learned over the years, is that not everyone will be in your life forever. As much as you may want them to be and as much as you both have been a staple in each other's lives for years, they may not be able to travel with you as you continue your journey, and you must be okay with knowing that. Accept it for what it is.

I am sure you both shared many laughs and many cries together. There comes a time when some friendships fade and that is just how things go. There should be no hard feelings and should be no love lost. Growing sometimes means growing apart.

People often do not want to let go. They are like me. They become hung up on all the years of friendship and dwell on all the energy that they have put these relationships or friendships. They are truly invested. Cutting off a friendship is truly one of the hardest things for me to do. Much harder than ending a romantic relationship. If you ask any of my exes, they will tell you that I am pretty good at that.

For me, I believe it is tough because I value loyalty and friendship. I consider all my friends to be family. But there truly comes a time when the relationship no longer serves a purpose in your life. Whether you have outgrown the person, or circumstances have changed, it is okay to change as well. To embrace what is going to transpire in your new season. Being comfortable does not hurt. It always feels rights. But growing, now that requires pain.

Getting out of the comfort zone may look like leaving someone behind. As you continue to grow, remember just like watching a garden blossom, not everything grows during the same season and not everything grows as fast. While you are shooting to the sky in the spring and your roots are digging deep into the earth, someone you are closest to, may just be beginning to bud and unfortunately you cannot pull them to where you are. When it is their time, they will soon see the light.

Half the Formula

With prayer, and no work, you only have half the formula. People come to me, as a sounding board and often for advice. They complain about or explain, depending on the situation, their disappointment, or their frustrations. They are looking to me for assistance.

Most times, they really are looking to me for the answer; for me to tell them what to do. I am not a licensed therapist. I express to people that I will not tell them what to do with their lives, because if they take my advice and it does pan out how it was intended to, I refuse to be held responsible.

As I began to have more of those conversations, I realized that people were expecting things that they were not ready for or that they were unsure of. They truly already knew the answer, they simply wanted to talk it through with someone. That is completely fine. The issued was that they had already made up their mind on whatever it was that they wanted. They just wanted reassurance.

So, the calls, most times, were more to have someone onboard with the decision that they had already made. The calls soon slowed down, when people realized that I was always going to give it to them straight and would never, under any circumstance, agree with something that I did not think would provide them with the best outcomes in the situation.

I always encouraged people to pray on their decisions, even if it was a simple thing, before they committed to it. Pray that it be in God's will and pray that it is what is honestly best for you. But praying can be two-fold. Often, people are praying for things to go in their favor. Your prayer really should be asking God to take control of the situation and asking that if it be in his will, that it come to fruition.

The other part is that people find themselves praying and then go right back to doing what they were doing before the prayer, making no efforts for change. They are not allowing change to manifest in their situation. You cannot use half the formula. We all need to be doing both. The great news is this can be applied to any situation. We must do the work, in every aspect. With no work, you will receive little to no results.

For years, I had not done all the work I needed to do after my traumatic youthful experiences. At the time, I honestly did not know that there was work that needed to be done. I would pray to God thanking him for keeping my family and me daily. For a while I was simply just praying to say.

I was not expecting anything from my prayers. I was just being thankful and asking that God continue to protect me. As I began my journey of self-work, I realized that there was a lot that I needed to do, including situations that I needed God to intervene on.

I first needed to start with acknowledging my traumas. Calling them what they were and discontinuing refusing to talk about them. I needed to label the feelings I had concerning my experiences. The feelings that I had bottled up, would be the type of feelings to appear and manifest in many ways over time.

They began to look like, not being able to trust people and preventing them from getting too close. They looked like, not wanting to be vulnerable in a relationship for the fear that I would become weak again. They looked like, not expressing myself when I did not like how I was being treated by someone and neglecting to address them when I felt like they were not present for me when I needed them.

Lord knows how these things were affecting me in my relationships and my friendships. When I began praying for my own well-being and acknowledging that I had a lot to do, I was able to consider that I needed to get to work. There was a lot I needed to do in order to combat some of my inner demons that no one was going to want to deal with, including myself.

Do not be defined by your past experiences. Embrace them. Accept them for what they are and use them as steppingstones to get to where you want to be on your life journey. There are some people who have a very hard time with trauma. Sometimes the experiences are so devasting that it might take a lot more than someone else to overcome them.

If this is you, keep pushing. My goal is never to shame anyone. It is to help you to understand that what has happened to you, does not have to consume you, disable you or dictate the life that you are destined to have. I encourage you to reach out to others, who you know have gone through similar experiences. Take time to practice self-care and give your body what it needs. Make sure to pray and to also give yourself grace, but do not give up.

We chose what defines us. We tend to embrace the great attributes about us and neglect the undesirable ones. I encourage you to respect and appreciate all the things that make you, you.

Acknowledging everything about you, gives you the ability to not allow anything, directly or indirectly, to define you. Also, recognizing that somethings should not be given much space in your life. They honestly do not deserve to. Think about the pain, trauma or negative thoughts and feelings you have neglected over the years. Now consider the many ways they have presented themselves, subconsciously, over the years and the affect that might have had on certain situations in your life.

I know my traumas absolutely did. There was no way that I could do my self-work without going back all those years and identifying how many of my past experiences shaped me. It is hard, but it is worth it.

Do yourself the ultimate favor and do not use half the formula. Do all the work that is required to ensure that you are walking in your best and truest self. Recognize that we truly are blessed to continue to wake up every day and have continuous opportunities to get it right.

A gentle reminder: self-work is also a journey, not a destination. The work must be consciously done every single day. Every day builds the habit that you truly need. You are your greatest investment, and you should make sure that you invest as much time in yourself as you can.

There is no recommended dosage, per se, but I do strongly encourage daily. It could look different for everyone. Maybe it is working out, maybe it is reading, or writing, meditating, praying, taking long baths, having uninterrupted morning coffee, studying the stock market, knitting, or singing. Whatever it is for you, take it and make it your thing. But give back to yourself. Take the power back from whoever, or whatever has it and reclaim your power. You deserve at least that.

Black and Blue

When I was fourteen years old, I wanted to be a probation officer. I had known young men around the city that were unfortunately under supervision and the duty of the job, sounded rewarding. Helping young men and women find resources in the community to be successful was right up my "I want to help everyone" alley.

I was beginning to recognize the differences of those who somehow ended up in the criminal justice system. Some people had limited opportunities and resources to begin with, so they decided to take matters into their own hands to level the playing field for themselves and their families. Some people simply took a misstep or ended up in the wrong place at the wrong time. Others were targeted again and again by local law enforcement due to fitting some description, while some people, truly just had a knack for criminal behavior and noncompliance.

I was offered my dream job at twenty-five. When I received the call, offering me the position, I honestly could not believe it. I was joining the government at such a young age and it felt unreal. I was shocked, more so, that I had been chosen over hundreds of people who had applied for this position. I knew that I was qualified for the position, but I initially still could not believe that I had been chosen.

I ended the phone call with my new Chief and sat outside my current job, at the time, digesting the news I had just received. This was not just what I had continued to pray for, but this was my dream coming to fruition. All the hard work I had put in over the years, all the tears I had cried in frustration and all the praying I did in hopes that I would be recognized for my accomplishments one day. Here I was, ready to take on the world by storm. Of course, they wanted me, how could they not.

I joined my colleagues in my new position, with this feeling of accomplishment and honor. I was feeling elated. I was ready and willing to serve and assist in ensuring the safety of my community and everything that came with it. I was excited to be a part of something so great, so noble and so rewarding. I felt like I had truly made it and I still do. I am obsessed with my job and I am honored to be a black female in law enforcement.

For as far back as most of us can remember, there has always been tension between the black community and law enforcement. Growing up, all my black male friends and past boyfriends all had stories to share of the way they were treated by the police and by law enforcement officials. Nine times out of ten, it was negative experiences.

Many of them had not had positive experiences with probation staff either. I vowed to always make sure that everyone I encountered, no matter race, skin tone, ethnicity, gender, economic class, or any other identifier, that they always had a positive experience with me. I wanted people to know that there are people in the criminal justice sector that look like them and that care about them. That there is someone on the other side of the table who understands them, who grew up in the same communities as them (or their family members) and who they can relate to. I do not want to take away from the officers and law enforcement officials who can relate while not being black, but there is something different about knowing the level to which someone can understand you.

Over the next few years, the tension between law enforcement and the black community had begun to rise dramatically. Black men and women were being murdered by the hands of men and women in law enforcement. These conversations were all over the news, now more than ever, with smartphones and body cameras capturing encounters and social media making these videos easy to share.

I do carry a weapon. A weapon that I am expected and mandated to spend numerous hours of training on how to use. As the tension increased, management in my organization made sure that we were always kept abreast of any changes, most importantly, the ones that might affect us. Unfortunately for us, the dust did not settle. Law enforcement officers began to become targets of upset persons out of anger and frustration.

Being a law enforcement officer, I knew this meant I needed to be more strategic and cautious regarding who I shared my employment with. I elected to refrain from certain conversations with people, in order not to spark any unwanted or unnecessary heated discussions. As a black woman, I understood that this meant I needed to be a little more vigilant than I already was. Being a woman, I always had to be on guard anyway.

The combination of all three factors, law enforcement official, being black, and being a woman, had my anxiety continuing to build. I naturally tried my hardest to stay clear of conversations and debates regarding law enforcement and misconduct since my view sometimes could be skewed and not always understood or received well by those who are not in law enforcement. I do have many thoughts and opinions regarding all that is transpiring around me daily; however, I am selective with who I share these with. It is not my job to defend anyone and it is rare that I ever do. I do defend my training and how sometimes, even that does not translate well with the community.

With the increase of unarmed black men and women being murdered, and the beginning of a worldwide pandemic, the murder of another unarmed black man shook the nation. What transpired next, will be documented in history books. Being black in law enforcement has not always been easy for many of us, but now, it was even tougher on those of color in law enforcement. My anxiety began to climb to a new high.

While my cousins, my son, and I quarantined together, we watched on television while all over the nation, people protested for black lives to matter and for the police to be defunded. Law enforcement was heavily targeted at this time, and I felt the furthest thing from safe. I began to have racing thoughts when I went for a run outside, feeling unsafe to be doing so without carrying a firearm.

I was afraid to have unintended conversations with anyone because there was never a guarantee where the conversation would go. I had people on one side telling me that I needed to stand with my black and brown people while others reminding me that I still carried a badge. I was feeling painfully trapped between being black by design and blue by choice.

After the first night of the protests, I slept with a heavy heart. My mind was racing with all that was transpiring around me. I was well into my sleep when my dreams crept in.

***

I was outside. It was dark. I was in a full-on sprint, running through the streets. Commotion and chaos were all around me. My surroundings were like what you might see in an action move, where the world is falling apart around the main character and they are trying to make it to safety. It was loud. I stopped and hid low, with my back up against a wall. My chest was heaving in and out as I struggled to catch my breath. My eyes were darting in every which direction. I was running for my life. It was unclear what or who was chasing me. There was panic in my eyes and sadness in my heart. I was being chased and I was unsure whether I was being hunted because I was black or because I was law enforcement.

***

I woke up clutching my chest, afraid and panicked. I reminded myself that it was just a dream, although it felt like reality. At some point I was able to drift back off to sleep.

The next morning when I woke up, the first thing I attempted to do was decipher my dream. Having a dream this vivid and with such heightened emotion, I realized this was a result of psychological stress. In the middle of a global wide pandemic, I was barely leaving the house to begin with, but now it felt like I was fighting against everything and everyone leaving the house. Take all my thoughts, feelings, emotions, and stressors and then add to that, being the mother of a black son living in the inner city. Whew.

The struggle of wanting your son to live a somewhat normal life but also knowing that he could be targeted by anyone, including law enforcement, for any reason or for no reason at all. My heart is heavy with even the thought of my son having to deal with what I know is inevitable. I have tried to shelter him as much as possible, but as he enters his teenage years, my fear and desire to protect him increase. I see how black men are treated from both my black and my blue lens and I want nothing more for my son to be viewed from a neutral lens.

My career has shifted my perspective in many ways; some positive and some not so much. I recognize that there are some people who deliberately look for trouble, so to speak, and others who suggest that they just cannot stay away from trouble. But there are also those who are targeted, mistreated or ended up in the wrong place, or with the wrong people, at the wrong time.

As the mother to a black teenage young man, I see how the media portrays those who look like my son. I see how law enforcement interacts with those who look like my son. I see the upward battle that my son will soon have to fight. He has no idea. It more than likely will not hit him, until he is stopped for the first time by law enforcement and told that he looks like someone that fits "the description" or that he "looks suspicious." He does not know that nonblack woman will fear him just because. Or that people will either expect him to play basketball, sell drugs or have gone to jail.

I must educate my son on how cruel the world can be. Reminding him not to speed late at night or to draw too much unnecessary attention to himself. To always call me if he does encounter law enforcement. To allow me to vet all his friends, and the females that he is interested in, so that I can try my best to ensure that he will not end up in situations that he may not be able to get himself out of.

The anxiety of even letting him out of the house to hang out with his friends is very real. The fear of him not making it back home from going to the store, or going to work, or even just being out for the run. The trauma runs deep for all of us black men and women.

If you did not feel like the pain and heartache before the pandemic, it was heightened and highlighted during the pandemic. And now, it seems hard to turn off. It is not just about being a great and educational parent, or a loving and supportive girlfriend or wife. It is about praying harder than you ever have done before because that is truly the only thing that is going to protect your loved one when they are not home.

My Prayer

I was not joking when I proclaimed that I was not going to give out my prayer for my fiancé. Do not get me wrong, there was plenty of praying, but ninety percent of the praying was for myself. It was quite frankly begging God that he would ensure that I was ready when my husband came. There was a lot of me asking God to keep me focused on myself and to not lose sight of my goals. To not stray from the plan that God had for me.

For nearly four years, before meeting my fiancé, I went through so many stages with waves of emotions while I was single. From sadness and loneliness to happiness and freedom. There were days I was accepting of my singleness and days I longed for nothing more than to be in a relationship. I travelled, I spent time with my friends, I shopped often, and I did as I pleased. I realized at some point during my singleness that I wanted to have a fun, and a lot of it, and that I did not need a partner to do so. I was truly all I needed.

It was after I had gotten all my singleness out, that I then allowed myself to date with a purpose. This form of "dating with a purpose" was not to be in a relationship, however. So, let me explain.

Dating with a purpose, at this point in my singleness, played a unique role in my life. Somewhere within year two of my singleness, I drafted a list. It was not a long grocery list as if I had not shopped in a month. The list was comprised of only seven items. Think of it as my main ingredients. Not all of them were hard deal breakers, but there sat a list of what I truly believed I needed in a future husband to ensure both of our continued happiness.

There was room for compromise on the list, but there was also a lot that I had left off the list. That is what the dating was for. Identifying what was not on the list, that could be thought of as negotiable or bonuses. That is what I spent the last two years of my singleness doing. Figuring out what exactly I wanted from my future husband; what I could and could not live without.

So, when my fiancé came looking for me, he checked off plenty of boxes and several negotiable boxes too. At the time, I did not know if I was truly ready to be in a relationship, let alone to be married. There was something else that I grappled with while I was single. It was not until my last year of my singleness that I was even willing to fall in love again.

After heartbreak and failed relationships, I was not interested in falling in love. I struggled with being that deeply attached to someone again. So deeply attached that it would leave me susceptible to be hurt again in the worst way. This was really what I was praying for. I was praying that God would open my heart to the right person. That I would be ready and willing when we met. I also prayed that he would be ready too.

When our love story initially began, one of the first things my fiancé revealed to me, was that he was ready to be married. From then on, this was a different "dating with a purpose". This was, for the first time, a road to marriage. We risked our lives through a worldwide pandemic, we supported each other through trying times and belly laughed through some of the most rewarding times. We built an amazing, incredible and unbreakable bond all while living in separate states and through times of uncertainty and civil unrest we loved on each other hard.

For me, there was no specific prayer for my fiancé; however, I prayed every single night that God would prepare me for what was in store. I prayed that if my wants list aligned with what God had planned for me, that he would present me with a man who could bring the list to fruition. That this man would honour and respect me and that he would be my husband.

There were plenty of instances where I thought I was ready to be married. In hindsight, I was not. I always dated with the initial confidence that the man I was dating would be my last. I soon learned I had to discontinue putting stock into these men. Some of them were unsure whether marriage was even in their future. And honestly, marriage may have been, it just may not have been with me. I realized I needed to become more upfront with the men I would date. I needed to be more intentional about our conversations even before the initial date. This way, I would not continue wasting my time.

As a female, wasted time delays not only our marriage timeline, but our childbearing timeline as well. Years spent; you cannot get back. When you are younger, you do not always recognize when someone is intentionally wasting your time. You are still figuring out how dating goes. You are happy and comfortable with how things are going. Maybe you all are going on regular dates and spending nights together. Maybe you are even taking trips together and have met each other's families. But now, three or four years later and there has been no serious conversation regarding solidifying your future together. Now you have just lost time. You are young, so no loss there.

But then, it happens again, and again, and you continue to allow yourself to basically be taken advantage of, because there is no commitment in the end. More wasted time. Yes, these are learning years for your final stop on your road to marriage, but it is all the giving that leaves you exhausted and bitter. Some of it we do to ourselves ladies.

Sometimes while being in a relationship, people tend to deny parts of themselves. The parts that want to party more, travel more, demand more from their partner, or feel free to be completely and unapologetically them. They do not want to tip the scale in the relationship or have their partner making assumptions about them. The goal is to always look like "marriage material." It is a façade. If a man truly loves you and considers marrying you, you should never have to dim your light or not feel comfortable to be yourself. He should embrace who you are and love you for every part of you.

When my fiancé found me, emotionally I was still unsure I wanted to love again, mentally I did not want to have to worry about another person and financially I was still cleaning up the mess I had made in my early twenties. But when my fiancé entered my life and showed me that loving him would be easy and would feel just right, I knew that I could love again.

God had presented me with a man who would love me for every part of me and treat me how I always should have been treated. God's plan is always a perfect plan. So, if you are looking for a prayer, pray that you are ready. Ask God to reveal to you what you need to work on. Pray that God will help you to be emotionally and mentally available, ready and willing and not desperate. You are asking God for your forever partner. Pray that you will be strong enough and prepared to say *no* to those who do not align with your list and God's plan.

By working on yourself, you are walking into your next relationship fully prepared. Or, if you are already in a relationship, you are building personal awareness and a stronger bond with the person you are with. By acknowledging your faults, your shortcomings, and your insecurities you can find ways to combat them and make positive change that will reflect in your day to day and in your relationship. You should be walking in a positive light. You should not be settling for less than you deserve. And ladies and gentlemen, it is perfectly fine to be single and to remain single until the man or woman that God has for you arrives.

Being single truthfully is the best way to work on yourself. You have ample time to do the work without being clouded by someone else's judgment or opinions. You can have a clear mind and think about the relationship that is going to bring you the most joy.

If you are in a relationship, continue to pray every night. Pray that God shows you whether this is the person you are supposed to be with and do not ignore the signs. If there are continuous question marks surrounding the person, then you should know they are not the one.

Pray often and pray for yourself. Do not ask God to make anyone the person for you. If they did not come the person for you, they are not the person for you. Many of us do not want to start over, but I can attest that you would rather start over with the right person than to stay somewhere with the wrong person; allowing yourself to potentially miss your blessing. You may then begin to exhibit feelings of resentment and may even feel trapped. We only get one shot at life, so take it.

In this New Decade

I made it to thirty. To a new decade, to a new way of life, and to a new outlook. My previous aches and pains are still there. They cannot be erased or forgotten; however, they cannot, will not, and have not defined me. They have given me some foundation, some grit, and somethings to be eternally grateful for. My past has made me, me. Every good part and every imperfect part.

As I reminisce over the years, it has become apparent that I may have been the only person who had not realized that my story made me a statistical phenomenon. It was my life that I was living day in and day out. It was not until many years later that I finally had a solid reflection. I, for the first time, had sat with myself. I thought of all my traumatic experiences and all the times I could have and maybe should have given up.

Fortunately for me, giving up was not something I was ever taught. There is no stopping me once I set my mind to something. I truly hope that everyone gains this level of drive and confidence.

These days, the magnitude of my accomplishments have become more real to me. Not just to me, but to others around me.

In those moments that I laid on my bedroom floor, waiting for what felt like my inevitable death, I did not think that I would be here today. There are people in my life who remind me often, that I was not supposed to be here. I was not supposed to be living this testimony.

Having my son at seventeen had its implications that I would not even graduate high school. But graduating from high school and then twice from the collegiate level, some people simply cannot image. How I climbed out of my depressive state and was strong enough to separate myself from a toxic relationship, without completely losing myself, is still something I am forever grateful for.

There were many times I wanted to strive less and be happy with a simple life. But my determination and drive for success would not allow me to. Some nights I would stay awake and stare at the ceiling in the dark. I knew where I needed to be, and I was trying to draw the line to get me there. Prayer was the most comforting those nights.

Only God knows how I was able to give my son the childhood he deserved. From Christmas' to birthday parties and overnight summer camps, while I struggled some days to keep it all together. I somehow managed to have the time and energy to be there for my friends whenever they needed me.

As I sit and reflect on my life in my thirtieth year, I am justly proud of myself. I have come a long way. To know that I have overcome so much and to still be strong enough to tell my story.

In this new decade, I look forward to all that my life is going bring. All the challenges, all the transition and all the excitement. For someone who has accomplished so much, my goal list continues to grow. Success is a journey and not a destination.

Rightfully so, thirty has been my breakthrough year. I longed for thirty. I was ready for thirty. I knew all that I was putting out into the universe and what it might cost me when the universe delivered. Thirty reminds me how young I still am and how much I still want to accomplish. Thirty feels like a reset. It feels like all my learned lessons, all my grandmother's prayers and all my creative energy colliding. Thirty has me investing in myself in more ways than one.

There was so much hype around the year 2020. The new decade was to be known as the year of vision; 20/20 vision. The vision board parties were at an all-time high towards the end of the previous decade. The goal lists were fully stacked, and mindsets were ready to be refreshed and reset.

When the pandemic hit, many people lost their vision. While some of them lost family members, jobs and dreams. They were so clouded by all that was around them, that the vision they once had was quickly stripped away. This change of events due to the pandemic, was tough on almost everyone. Loss continued to increase and for some people every day they were on the brink of a mental health crisis. We all had different mechanisms that helped us to keep pushing through.

When the clouds had begun to break, and people began to understand and acknowledge this new norm that we were all living in, some people had a hard time shifting or doing well under stress. So, when their vision board began to fall apart, they never thought to add new pieces or simply just move the pieces around. My vision was still there; however, I could see that others had shifted their focus.

Many people that I know, now had the ability to work from home. So many companies that once said that employees could never work remote, set their employees up expeditiously with remote access to ensure that productivity continued. This was one of the golden keys of the pandemic and the 20/20 year. This transition brought freedom and flexibility.

Some people took this as an opportunity to switch careers. Realizing that this was the best time to seek additional employment opportunities. Another nugget here. Learning what you do not want and going after what will make you happy.

Many people were able to save and pay off debt, like myself. Others were able to study the stock market and finally begin to make informed decisions on trading. Some people opted to have a small wedding and get married and others got engaged.

So many life changing events: starting businesses, having children, picking up hobbies. Through a worldwide pandemic, people's eyes were open wide to where they were in life, and hopefully to where they want to be. They were recognizing what and who were most important in their lives.

I tell people, if I did not risk my life during a worldwide pandemic to see someone, that suggests how we both value our relationship. The vision was not what many people thought or hoped it was going to be, but I am a believer that it was the vision that we all needed. We all needed a break. We cannot be our best selves with continued clouded visions.

Mental health ran high, people became unemployed, and lost family members. I am not negating any of those terrible outcomes; however, I would like for people to consider something. The world stopped. For the first time in a long time, it stopped. It gave us all time to be with family, but most importantly to be with ourselves. To let our minds, wander, to consider where we are in our lives.

For me, it was perfect. After I worked through the initial fear and anxiety, of course. It was my last year in my twenties and it brought me so much clarity. I now had the time to do everything that I wanted to do. I did not have my hour commute in the mornings anymore which meant that my early mornings belonged to me. I would go for a run on my lunch break. I could fit grocery shopping and laundry into a break in my day and could spend much needed time with my son.

It became a completely different world for me and ultimately a game changer. My body began waking up earlier; I discontinued using an alarm clock. I now had time, undivided for myself. I knew that it was time to begin feeding my passion.

My passion, since a young girl has always been to help others. I tend to be known as the mother of my friend groups. The nourishing spirit and the one who gives good advice; I also am the one who will tell you when you are wrong.

With this spirit, comes the need and desire to help guide others. That was my initial drive to become a probation officer. But deep down inside there was always a desire to help others who looked just like me. Young black females who carried trauma around in their knapsacks and had no idea what to do with it. Those truly are the people who have my heart. Why?

I felt like I always had to figure things out alone. I did not know anyone going through the traumas that I had gone through at the same time I was faced with them. So, I was alone. I took every one of my traumatic experiences and I tucked it away and continued to strive. I was not going to let anything keep me from the life I had envisioned for myself. Defense mechanism? Possibly. Or, it could have also been not having anyone to turn to; anyone who could give me proper guidance because they had not experienced what I had.

It was not until I was in my late twenties that I realized that I had a voice. That I could speak out and let other young women know that they are not alone. That they have places to seek refuge. There is a trauma tribe, and it may not be within your friend circle and that is fine. But the more of us women that remain silent and do not speak about our pains, risk us carrying these burdens for far longer than we should. We allow the trauma to continue to affect us on so many different levels.

The self-work begins now and will continue for the rest of your life. Self-work is truly an ongoing commitment with unlimited benefits. Having the ability and foresight to begin sooner, will alleviate so much heartache. It can prevent so many lessons and mishaps down the line.

The most effective way I believed that I could use my passion to touch many on a broader scale, was to begin writing on my blog. The feedback that I received ensured me that writing this mini memoir would allow me to help so many from all over who share similar stories. There was outpour of women who related to many posts that I had shared. In a world where we are expected to continuously look like we have it all together, sadly, many of us are falling apart. I turned to my passion and I will forever be grateful for this outlet.

When I was young Tai, who wanted to be a doctor when she grew up, I had no idea the journey that awaited me. This journey has been an eventful one, to say the least. When I went through my traumatic experiences, I put it all outside of my mind so that I could move on. Feel normal and look the part. When I was single for those four years, I did the most self-work I have ever done in my life.

I have always tried to use my situations and circumstances as lessons. Maybe lessons I have never wanted to learn, but lessons that have allowed me to grow to be the woman that I am today. I am truly grateful that God saw more for my life and continues to call on me to use my life as a true testimony.

To the Reader

Thank you for taking this journey with me. Deciding to write this mini memoir brought its own rollercoaster of emotions. Committing to writing this took a lot of digging deep and reminding myself to be expressive. I am grateful. For someone as private as me and not as emotionally open, I had to constantly remind myself that the only way I could truly be helpful, is to be completely vulnerable. I wanted all of you to not just read what I had to say, but to *feel*. I cried many times during my writing sessions. Writing this mini memoir has truly been a form of therapy for me. It has allowed me to really recognize how far I have come. I genuinely hope that this writing can help someone who needs some motivation, encouragement, or a pep-talk. I am thankful for the continued love and encouragement and I hope this writing truly, finds you well.

Here's to you,
Tai

Made in the USA
Middletown, DE
20 October 2022

13007891R00073